How To B

K. M. RYAN Copyright © 2012 K. M. Ryan

ISBN-10: 1475170076

ISBN-13: 978-1475170078

DEDICATION

To Tom and Bonnie who are best friends, and the best parents ever.

CONTENTS

1 Romantic Bedroom Ideas

These romantic bedroom ideas offer adult romance ideas and romantic night ideas for couples.

♥ "500 Lovemaking Tips and Secrets". Read it together.

♥ Do art drawings of each other - in the nude.

♥ Install a fireplace. Snuggle in bed watching the romantic glow.

♥ Keep massage oil on the nightstand. If either wants a massage, you're ready!

♥ Make your own planetarium at home by buying glow in the dark stars and putting them on the ceiling of your bedroom.

♥ Once a month, turn off the phones, tv, computer and lights. Snuggle together in bed with candlelight and talk about whatever you want to talk about for at least one hour.

♥ Read "1000 Questions For Couples" together. Try answering one question every day when you go to bed or when you get up.

♥ Remove the lightbulbs in the bedroom lamps and put candles around the room.

♥ Scatter rose petals over the bed.

♥ Try chocolate body paints.

♥ Turn the radio on in your bedroom and slow dance together. Whisper romantic words to each other.

♥ Be sensual.

♥ Do a strip tease for each other.

♥ Get a "do not disturb" sign.

♥ Guys, wear a pair of silk boxers.

♥ Hang a piece of romantic art on the wall.

♥ Keep mistletoe hung in your bedroom all year.

♥ Keep a romantic love song cd in your room.

♥ Make sure your bedroom door has a lock.

♥ Play charades.

♥ Play show and tell.

♥ Play strip poker.

♥ Play truth or dare.

♥ Play twister in the nude.

♥ Practice open communication regarding your intimate needs and wants.

♥ Get a dimmer switch installed for the lights.

♥ Get a down comforter.

♥ Get a feather bed.

♥ Guys, pretend to be a Chippendale.

♥ Keep a book in your nightstand drawer by a sexpert.

♥ Play Scrabble with romantic words only.

♥ Put a mirror on the ceiling.

♥ Put lace panels around your bed.

♥ Put satin sheets on the bed. Buy 2 sets, one in her favorite color and one in his favorite color.

♥ Read a Dr. Ruth book.

♥ Read the "Joy of Sex".

♥ Set your radio to a romantic, soft music station.

♥ Buy a canopy bed.

♥ Buy a 4 poster bed.

♥ Buy heart shaped doilies for the nightstand.

♥ Buy one set of pajamas in his size. Ladies wear the top and men wear the bottoms.

♥ Frame your wedding invitation and hang it up.

♥ Get books on cd or tape that are romantic. Listen to it each night in bed.

♥ Have your own private lingerie party for him. Try on the new outfits you bought.

♥ If your love can't sleep, get up with them and keep them company or rub their back or temples.

♥ Keep some Mozart music in your night stand drawer.

♥ Leave a trail of chocolate Kisses from the door to the bedroom where you will be waiting happily for your sweetie.

♥ Paint a mural on a wall.

♥ Practice loosening inhibitions.

♥ Put a lava lamp on your night stand.

♥ Put an oil lamp in your room.

♥ Put lace curtains up.

♥ Put up a ceiling fan.

♥ Recreate your favorite movie love scene together.

♥ Sing to her as you cuddle in bed.

♥ Sleep in the nude.

♥ Slowly undress each other.

♥ Snuggle together under an electric blanket.

♥ Spoon.

♥ Switch sides of the bed you sleep on occasionally.

2 Inexpensive Romantic Ideas

These inexpensive romantic ideas offer cheap romantic ideas, good date ideas, and adult romance ideas that won't break the bank.

♥ At Halloween, tour a local haunted house. Stay close to her and hug her if she screams.

♥ At the local fair, try to win her a stuffed animal.

♥ Buy matching shirts and wear them together occasionally.

♥ Buy one piece of your sweetie's favorite dessert and split it with him or her. Even if it's not your favorite, try it because your sweetie likes it.

♥ Carve a pumpkin together.

♥ Color Easter eggs together.

♥ Each hide some Easter eggs, then look for them together.

♥ Fly a kite together. Help her assemble hers and get it in the air.

♥ Get a paint by numbers kit. He does odd number painting and she does even numbers.

♥ Go fishing together, bait the hook for her and help her reel in her catch.

♥ Go on a hayride together. Bring her a thermos of apple cider.

♥ Go out for a green beer on St. Patrick's Day.

♥ Go to a church festival and play bingo together.

♥ Go to an amusement park at night and ride the ferris wheel. Check out the lights as you're up on top.

♥ Go to karaoke and sing each other a romantic song.

♥ Go to the amusement park, get on the bumper cars and ram each other (not too hard!).

♥ Go to the store, buy seed packets and start a garden together.

♥ Go to your city's farmer's market and buy fresh fruit and veggies together.

♥ Have a water balloon fight.

♥ Hold hands and walk through a corn maize.

♥ If one of you likes apple pie, go to an orchard, pick apples together, then come home and bake a pie for the one who likes it (or do it together).

♥ If you have a pool, have a pool date. Swim together, snuggle on a raft, call and order pizza and dine by the water.

♥ Make each other up an Easter basket with each other's favorite treats.

♥ Over the summer, go to the lake or ocean once a month. Watch the people, de-stress by the water and enjoy your favorite picnic lunch.

♥ Put together puzzles.

♥ Rent a bicycle built for two.

♥ Ride the merry go round together. Get on separate horses side by side and hold hands.

♥ Start a coin collection together.

♥ Start a stamp collection together.

♥ Stop in the photo booth at the mall for some fun pictures of the two of you.

♥ Blow bubbles together. See who can make the biggest bubble.

♥ Cut love quotes out of magazines and newspapers. Make a collage and hang it up.

♥ Eat a foot long hot dog together. Each start at the opposite end.

♥ Go to an auction together.

♥ Go to a book signing together.

♥ Go to a tea café. Have your favorite tea and maybe a muffin or dessert.

♥ Go to your high school's home football games. Share a blanket and some hot dogs and cocoa.

♥ Make a family tree together.

♥ Read a book on body language together.

♥ Set up a lemonade stand together. Give it away for free.

♥ Take your child's Etch a Sketch and write "I love you."

♥ Using spaghetti or licorice, each put one end in your mouth then when your lips meet, kiss.

♥ Wake up early to catch the sunrise. Take your sweetie out to an early morning breakfast afterwards.

♥ Watch the fireworks together on July 4th. Bring a snack along to enjoy.

♥ Break a popsicle in half and share it.

♥ Bring her one flower to wear in her hair.

♥ Buy a journal with flowers or hearts on it. This is your romantic journal. Both of you can write something every day. After a date together, write what you loved about the date. Or write something nice about your sweetie.

♥ Buy his and her Pez dispensers.

♥ Buy some plastic Easter eggs that pull apart. Write love notes and place them inside.

♥ Buy two goldfish and name them your pet names for each other.

♥ Buy your song in a foreign language and learn how to sing it.

♥ Collect post cards from your trips. Arrange them, frame the arrangement and hang it up.

♥ Create a new drink together. Make it your drink.

♥ Cut out romantic comics from the paper. Make a collage out of them and hang them up. Or save them in a photo album.

♥ Feed each other jello.

♥ Get a stamp with a heart or "love" on it at a craft store. Use it on your love notes and letters.

♥ Get a magnetic whiteboard for your refrigerator. Write love notes on it for each other.

♥ Get bandaids with hearts on them.

♥ Get checks with hearts on them.

♥ Get name labels with hearts on them.

♥ Have a tea party at home complete with stuffed animals to fill the empty chairs.

♥ If you're leaving on a trip without your love, mail a card to him or her one day before you leave that says how much you miss them.

♥ Learn foot reflexology..

♥ Make a collage from the cards you have received from each other.

♥ Make a quilt together.

♥ Make fresh orange juice for her.

♥ Prune one shrub into a heart shape.

♥ Put heart stickers on the remote control.

♥ Put heart stickers on your mailbox.

♥ Put sunscreen on each other.

♥ Put up a shower curtain with hearts on it.

♥ Rewrite "your song" in your own words. Sing it to your sweetie or frame the lyrics.

♥ Save one or two flowers from each bouquet your sweetie gives you to make a dried flower arrangement you can hang on the wall or put in a vase.

♥ Sign up for a charity walk together. Make a donation.

♥ Spell, "I love you" with toothpicks on the kitchen counter or table.

♥ Take a ride through the Tunnel of Love.

♥ Wish on coins thrown into a fountain.

♥ Write a love note on a candy bar wrapper.

♥ Write a love note on a gum wrapper.

♥ Write a romantic message on the kitchen counter with a can of spray cool whip.

3 Romantic Christmas Ideas

These romantic Christmas ideas will show you how to be romantic during the holiday season.

♥ There's inexpensive romantic ideas, free romance ideas and ideas for fun and quiet time together.

♥ Get into the holiday spirit and pick one or two of these romantic ideas as your own.

♥ Address Christmas cards together. One will write inside the card while the other addresses the envelopes.

♥ Bake her favorite cookies.

♥ Bake his favorite cookies.

♥ Be a kid again. Make garland to hang on the tree by cutting up different colored construction paper, folding into circles and connecting each piece together until you have a long chain.

♥ Buy a gift together then donate it to charity.

♥ Buy matching monogrammed Christmas ornaments and hang them on the tree together.

♥ Check out live nativity scenes.

♥ Decorate the Christmas tree together by taking turns placing ornaments on the tree, stringing lights and putting the garland on.

♥ Do a tour of homes in your town at Christmas.

♥ Drive around your town to check out the Christmas lights.

♥ Get 12 photos of yourself - growing up, high school or college graduations, when you were on vacation, with pets, with your kids or whatever else you think of. Get a calendar made up for the following year out of the pictures and give to your sweetheart on Christmas. You can also use one photo to personalize mugs and mouse pads, too!

♥ Go buy mistletoe, come home and put it up - kissing most of the time. Put it as many places as you can in your home and kiss when you both pass by.

♥ Go caroling.

♥ Go Christmas shopping together. Buy each other one gift that the other wants. Even though it's not a surprise, go home and wrap it anyway!

♥ Go Christmas tree shopping together.

♥ Go to a Christmas shop and pick out one trinket for each other to put in your house - or on the tree.

♥ Go to midnight Mass together.

♥ Go to Rockefeller Center to see their Christmas show.

♥ Go to the dollar store and pick out Christmas napkins and placemats you both like.

♥ Greet him at the door - with a smile and some bows on.

♥ Have Christmas stockings with each other's names on. Make sure Santa puts a few special surprises in each one.

♥ Head to the Christmas in July sales together.

♥ Keep track of Santa's whereabouts at Christmas as you drink hot cocoa and dream about your presents.

♥ Make cranberry garland for your tree.

♥ Make each other a Christmas ornament.

♥ Make garland out of popcorn. Eat some, string some.

♥ Make tasty gingerbread men and women together. Connect one pair's hands before you bake.

♥ One night during Christmas, turn everything off but the Christmas lights and snuggle on the couch together enjoying the beauty of the tree.

♥ Only have eyes for her at your company Christmas party.

♥ Play Christmas music together throughout the season and sing as loud as you can.

♥ Play footsies under the table at your Christmas party.

♥ Put milk and cookies out for Santa. If, in the morning, Santa hadn't eaten them because he was too full, enjoy them together before you open your gifts.

♥ Save one gift for each other until last minute. Head to the mall on December 24th, give each other one hour to buy one gift, then meet at the food court for a snack before you head home to wrap.

♥ Set up the train together, pop some popcorn and watch it go round and round together.

♥ Skip your date night one week at Christmas time and give that money to the Salvation Army.

♥ Take a sleigh ride together to see the homes decorated with lights.

♥ Watch a holiday movie together with some eggnog.

♥ Watch the tree lighting at Rockefeller Center.

♥ Write her name in the Christmas snow.

♥ Write his name in the Christmas snow.

♥ Be each other's secret Santa.

♥ Buy sets of heart shaped ornaments and use only those to decorate the tree.

♥ Buy his and her poinsettias. Keep them side by side.

♥ Buy matching Christmas sweaters.

♥ Do something romantic every day during the 12 days of Christmas.

♥ Get a Santa Claus suit. Have her sit on your lap and tell you what she wants for Christmas.

♥ Hang a necklace or bracelet on the Christmas tree and wait for your sweetie to find it.

♥ If you live some place that's cold on Christmas, go some place warm to spend the holiday.

♥ Make heart garland out of construction paper.

♥ Send your sweetie a Christmas card. Include a letter that highlights the past year and things the two of you did together.

♥ Share red and green jelly beans.

♥ Watch "Charlie Brown's" Christmas story together.

♥ Watch "Frosty the Snowman" together.

♥ Watch "Rudolph the Red Nose Reindeer" together.

4 Free Romance Ideas

These free romance ideas will give you some great date ideas and ideas for a fun date that won't cost anything!

Just as beauty is in the eye of the beholder, so is romance. Romance and romantic ideas mean different things to each couple.

Romance can be as simple as not what you're doing, but who you're doing it with.

♥ Audition together for your next home town theater's play.

♥ Beautify your town and help pick up litter.

♥ Browse a catalog and make your wish lists.

♥ Build a sand castle together at the beach.

♥ Clean out your closets and tell each other one outfit the other should keep. Keep these then give the rest to charity.

♥ Exercise together. Once a week, pick something you both enjoy and do it together (jogging, walking, bicycling). One of the free romance ideas that gets you together as a couple and also keeps you in shape.

♥ Get a book from the library and read it together.

♥ Go hiking and see how many different birds you can spot (and name).

♥ Go to a busy place and people watch.

♥ Go to a local pond or lake, bring bread and feed the ducks.

♥ Go to a parade together.

♥ Go to a state park for outdoor fun.

♥ Go to an art gallery and pick out your favorite paintings. Agree with your partner's choice and say why you like it, too.

♥ Go to the library together, pick out romantic books and read excerpts to each other.

♥ Go to the local park and swing side by side.

♥ Go to the ocean and pick seashells. Come home and put them and some sand in a glass jar. Display it as your beach souvenir.

♥ Go to your town's free concerts and hold hands while you sing and dance to the music.

♥ Go to your town's free outside movie nights.

♥ Hold hands as you walk together and window shop. You'll learn each other's tastes as you stop and admire things that catch your eye.

♥ If you have a ping pong table at home, play - the loser gives the winner a massage.

♥ If you have a pool table, play - the loser does what the winner wants for an hour or two.

♥ Kick off your shoes and wade in a fountain.

♥ Kiss at 11:59 PM New Year's Eve through 12:00 AM New Year's Day (1 minute!).

♥ Make up pet names for each other and use them.

♥ On a warm day when it's raining, take a hand in hand walk. Splash in puddles and share one umbrella.

♥ Play air hockey at home. When someone scores a point, kiss each other.

♥ Play badminton.

♥ Play frisbee together.

♥ Play hopscotch. The winner makes the loser's favorite treat.

♥ Play water basketball together.

♥ Go camping - in your backyard. Count the stars.

♥ Learn "I love you" in a foreign language and say it every day.

♥ Learn "I love you" in sign language and use this.

♥ Rake the leaves together then jump in them.

♥ Read a book from the library on male/female communication together.

♥ Read the comics together and laugh together.

♥ Ride the elevator and kiss at each floor stop.

♥ Stop by a youth baseball game and watch the kids play. Root for both teams.

♥ Take a drive in the Fall when the leaves are changing color.

♥ Take a drive through the country and watch for animals like deer.

♥ Take a nap together outside in your hammock.

♥ Visit colorful flower gardens.

♥ Volunteer somewhere together.

♥ Watch Punxsutawney Phil and predict whether he will see his shadow or not. Winner gives loser a massage or draws them a nice hot bath.

♥ Watch the Thanksgiving Day parade on tv together.

♥ When at a party, pretend the two of you just met and flirt the night away like star struck lovers.

♥ At a party, pretend you don't know each other. Use your best pick up lines on her.

♥ Attend a game show taping together.

♥ Attend a poetry reading together.

♥ Attend a talk show taping together.

♥ Browse in antique stores.

♥ Browse your wedding album together. Have your favorite drinks and reminisce.

♥ Check out covered bridges.

♥ Drive past your childhood homes.

♥ Eat a midnight snack together.

♥ Find waterfalls close to you then visit them.

♥ Make New Year's resolutions - one each, and help each other keep it.

♥ Make the screensaver read, "I love you".

♥ Pick wildflowers.

♥ Write romantic limericks.

♥ Ask to chaperone your alma mater's prom. Reminisce about your proms.

♥ At the next wedding you attend, feed each other wedding cake like the bride and groom do.

♥ At the next wedding reception you go to, request that "your song" be played.

♥ Blow kisses to each other.

♥ Call each other and talk in low, husky tones.

♥ Carve your initials in a tree on your property.

♥ Cool off with a hose fight. See who gets wet the quickest.

♥ Create a romantic motto together.

♥ Exchange business cards with each other. Write something romantic on the back.

♥ Find a place where it echoes and shout, "I love you".

♥ Go through revolving doors together.

♥ Go skinny dipping in the moonlight.

♥ If you have a talking bird, teach it to say, "I love you" with your name and also with your sweetie's name.

♥ Kiss at red lights.

♥ Learn how to gift wrap together.

♥ Make a screensaver out of a picture of the two of you.

♥ Make up free love coupons. These can be for hugs, kisses, foot massages, back rubs, breakfasts, lunches or dinners out, one week of chauffeuring the other around, one week of doing all the housework, a romantic weekend getaway, or anything you want to put on the coupon.

♥ On a hot day, sit under a shade tree together.

♥ Point out heart shaped clouds to your sweetie.

♥ Ride the escalator side by side holding hands.

♥ Sleep on your balcony.

♥ Sleep on your screened in patio like you were camping.

♥ Sort through your coins and save the ones with the year you were married.

♥ Stand underneath the lawn sprinkler together.

♥ Take a midnight walk.

♥ Take a walk in the fog.

♥ Talk baby talk to each other.

♥ Tell your sweetie how much he or she means to you by drawing pictures only, no words.

♥ Walk the boardwalk.

♥ Walk the dog together holding hands.

♥ Wash your hair in the rain.

♥ When you are exclusive or engaged, build a bonfire to burn all momentos of former loves.

♥ When your sweetie is going out of town, draw a map that leads your love back to your heart.

♥ Whisper sweet nothings in each other's ears.

♥ Wish on a falling star.

♥ Write a check to your sweetie for 1000 hugs, kisses, back rubs, foot rubs, or anything else you can think of.

♥ Write your relationship's mission statement and keep it prominently displayed.

5 Ideas For A Fun Date

Looking for ideas for a fun date?

These fun date ideas offer creative dating ideas like skydiving and balloon rides plus good date ideas for getting outdoors with your sweetie to taking a class together.

♥ Ball room dancing.

♥ Bowling (kiss each time one of you gets a strike).

♥ Bungee jumping.

♥ Get costumes and go trick or treating on Halloween together.

♥ Get pedicures together.

♥ Go 4 wheeling.

♥ Go see a rodeo.

♥ Go to a local art festival and have caricatures done of each other. Hang them side by side at home.

♥ Go to a planetarium together.

♥ Go to a sporting event.

♥ Go to a video arcade.

♥ Go to a zoo and feed the animals.

♥ Go to an aquarium.

♥ Go to dog shows and pick your favorite dog. If your dog is picked as a winner, your sweetie will treat you to your favorite food.

♥ Go to Gettysburg and tour the Battlefields. Stop at one of the cafes for a tasty lunch and latte.

♥ Go to a high school reunion together. You'll find out what you're sweetie was like then and meet their friends.

♥ Go to the circus.

- ♥ Go white water rafting.

- ♥ Have a special date every year on the day you first met.

- ♥ Helicopter tour in Hawaii.

- ♥ Hot air balloon ride.

- ♥ Jeep tour of the Grand Canyon.

- ♥ Learn a foreign language together - especially phrases like "I love you", "hug me", "you're hot" and "you're sexy".

- ♥ Parasailing.

- ♥ Rent a pontoon boat.

- ♥ Rock climbing.

- ♥ Scuba diving.

- ♥ Sign up for a few weeks of dance classes together.

- ♥ Skeet shooting.

- ♥ Skydiving.

- ♥ Snorkeling.

- ♥ Star in your own romance novel.

- ♥ Take a boat tour and whale and dolphin watch.

- ♥ Take a car repair class together.

- ♥ Take a chair lift ride together.

- ♥ Take a college class together and help each other with the homework.

- ♥ Take a cooking class together.

- ♥ Take a romantic vacation together.

- ♥ Take flying lessons together.

- ♥ Take a photography class together, take pictures of each other and present the other one with your present on each other's birthdays.

♥ Take a train ride through the mountains when the leaves are changing.

♥ Take music lessons together. Learn how to play your favorite song.

♥ Take tennis or golf lessons together.

♥ Try archery.

♥ Build a snow man together.

♥ For those in warm places, head to the beach when you hear how much snow other parts of the country got. And be glad you're some place fairly warm!

♥ Go ice skating or roller skating. If ice skating outside, secretly prepare a thermos of hot chocolate and surprise her.

♥ Go skiing.

♥ Go sled riding.

♥ Go snowboarding.

♥ Go snowshoeing.

♥ Go snowmobiling.

♥ Have a snow ball fight.

♥ Ice fishing.

♥ Make an ice sculpture.

♥ Make snow angels together.

♥ Take a walk holding hands right after a snow fall and be the first to make footprints.

♥ Get a can of colored spray paint. Write, "I love you" on the snow.

♥ Make snow sculptures.

♥ Share a cup of cocoa by candlelight.

♥ Trace a heart in the snow and put your initials inside.

♥ Build a tree house together.

♥ Check out a butterfly garden.

♥ Check out the Oscar Meyer Weinermobile when it comes to your city.

♥ Cut fun things the two of you would like to do out of magazines or the newspaper. Get a cork board from a craft store. Tape all the ideas on. Hang it up somewhere, get a dart and throw. Where the dart lands is what you will do for that date.

♥ Get the same tattoo. Or each get the other's name tattooed.

♥ Go skateboarding.

♥ Go to a beer festival.

♥ Go to a classic car show.

♥ Go to a flower show.

♥ Go to fashion shows.

♥ Go to a Trekkie convention.

♥ Have your portrait professionally taken

♥ Head to the Mall of America.

♥ Listen to a barbershop quartet.

♥ Ride a double decker bus in New York City.

♥ Build a bear together.

♥ Get your astrological charts done.

♥ Go horseback riding.

♥ Go on an African safari.

♥ Go surfing.

♥ Go water skiing.

♥ Have your handwriting analyzed.

♥ Rent a paddle boat.

♥ Ride the cable car in San Francisco.

♥ Start a "restaurant of the month" club. Each month, pick a different restaurant to go to.

♥ Take a ceramics class together.

♥ Visit a dude ranch.

♥ Attend a bull riding event.

♥ Get a makeover together.

♥ Go parachuting.

♥ Go to a Halloween party dressed up as a romantic couple from real life, the movies or comic strips.

♥ Have a picnic on your balcony.

♥ Have a picnic on your porch or patio that's screened in.

♥ Open IRAs together.

♥ Pick one holiday a month and do something related to the day. Make it fun! There's all kinds of unknown holidays you can choose!

♥ Ride a mechanical bull.

♥ Ride a rollercoaster.

♥ Start a romantic book club together with other couples. Meet once a month to discuss.

♥ Visit your colleges together.

6 Romantic Gifts For Her

If you're looking for birthday present ideas, romantic presents for an anniversary, ideas for unusual romantic gifts or cheap romantic gift ideas, you'll find those here.

♥ A bag of her favorite snack food with her favorite colored bow on it.

♥ A chocolate rose.

♥ A homemade birthday card.

♥ Book by her favorite author.

♥ Framed picture of the two of you.

♥ Go back and buy her something she liked but didn't buy for herself and give it to her on her birthday.

♥ Go shopping with her and pick out an outfit you like for her. Have her try it on. If she likes it, buy it.

♥ Her favorite bath gel, lotion and shampoo.

♥ Her favorite candy.

♥ Her favorite perfume.

♥ License plate with your pet name for her on it.

♥ One sexy lingerie item.

♥ Show your warm and fuzzy side by buying his and her matching and oh so soft robes. Wrap them both up and let her open it.

♥ Subscription to her favorite magazine.

♥ Take her for a champagne breakfast.

♥ A book signed by her favorite author.

♥ A heart key chain inscribed with "(your name) loves (her name)."

♥ A made to order watch with your picture on the watch face.

♥ A new piece to add to whatever she collects.

♥ Any gift you see that reminds you of her. When she opens it, tell her why you bought and and why you thought of her when you saw it.

♥ Charm bracelet. For the first charm, get a heart shaped charm and engrave it with both of your initials.

♥ Get a picture of the two of you. Turn this into a homemade birthday card for her.

♥ Gift certificate to her favorite hair salon.

♥ Gift certificate to a spa for a facial and to have her nails done.

♥ Have a balloon animal made for her (or do it yourself!).

♥ Her favorite flowers in her favorite color.

♥ Jewelry she likes - necklace, bracelet, earrings, ring in gold or silver, whatever she prefers. Have a necklace or bracelet inscribed with "I love you."

♥ Send her balloons that say "I love you."

♥ Take each letter of her first name and make a word out of it to describe how you feel about her. "Amy" could be adorable, magnificent, yummy! Use a marker on 8 1/2" x 11" paper with a pretty design (check craft stores). Using your best hand writing, write her name going down the left side of the paper, then write the rest of the word beside each letter. Frame it.

♥ A family ring.

♥ A framed copy of your marriage license.

♥ A mood ring.

♥ Assortment of her favorite tea.

♥ Flag with hearts.

♥ Gift certificate to her favorite coffee shop.

♥ Heart shaped door mat or kitchen rug.

♥ Heart shaped key chain with a piece missing. Attach a note that says, "You have a big piece of my heart".

♥ Heart shaped pillow embroidered with both sets of initials.

♥ Leather purse or key chain.

♥ Pick something from the Victoria's Secret catalogue. Lingerie, body lotion or perfume.

♥ Pretty hair ribbons and accessories.

♥ Six months of professional house cleaning services.

♥ Warm and fuzzy scarf and gloves.

♥ A book of romantic quotations. Write your own, or look for them throughout the year.

♥ A toy or game she loved when she was little.

♥ A year's membership in a flower of the month club.

♥ An angel figurine.

♥ Automatic car starter.

♥ Basket of her favorite gourmet treats.

♥ Bubble bath.

♥ Crystal wine glasses.

♥ Flavored lip gloss.

♥ Foot massager.

♥ Get an oil painting done from a picture of the two of you.

♥ Go to a perfume store where they create perfume. Create a unique perfume for her.

♥ Gold or silver hair brush and comb.

♥ Harlequin romance novels.

♥ Heart shaped locket with your picture.

♥ Heart shaped sachets.

♥ Heart shaped wind chimes.

♥ Kitchen gadgets in heart shapes.

♥ Lace socks.

♥ Lipstick in her favorite shades.

♥ Make a calendar with a different picture of you as a couple on each month. Write 1 romantic note on one date a month. Also, pick one date a month and tell her you will meet her for lunch or dinner on that day.

♥ Music box.

♥ Picture frame with frames side by side. Put both of your baby pictures in it.

♥ Pick out an outfit for her. Have the store put it on a mannequin with her name on a stickie name badge stuck to the outfit. Take her to the store and lead her to it.

♥ Sexy swimsuit.

♥ Silky slippers.

♥ Warm, fuzzy socks.

♥ What is her all time favorite romantic song? Once you find out, get the lyrics, have them written in calligraphy and frame it.

7 Romantic Gifts For Him

Ideas for romantic gifts for him. If you're looking for gifts for husbands or boyfriends, romantic birthday gift ideas, or creative romantic gift ideas look no further.

♥ A book signed by his favorite author.

♥ A new techie gadget he's been admiring.

♥ Book by his favorite author.

♥ Framed picture of his pet with a toy for the pet.

♥ Go golfing with him. Be the caddy and drive the golf cart. Then treat him to lunch.

♥ Go to a sports store and buy him his favorite team tee shirt, hat or sweatshirt - whatever he likes to wear.

♥ His favorite cologne.

♥ His favorite tools.

♥ If he normally wears boxers, buy him briefs and vice versa.

♥ License plate with his favorite team's name.

♥ License plate with your pet name for him on it.

♥ New remote control.

♥ Subscription to his favorite magazine.

♥ Tickets to a sporting event.

♥ A sports item signed by his favorite player.

♥ Balloons that say "You're sexy".

♥ Case of his favorite beer.

♥ Get a picture of the two of you. Look online and find where you can have this made into a 100 piece puzzle.

♥ Gift certificate to have his car washed and waxed.

♥ Gift certificate to his favorite sporting goods store.

♥ Gift certificate to Lowe's or Home Depot.

♥ Heart shaped paperweight in clear or blue.

♥ Jigsaw puzzle from a city you two visited together. You can help him put it together.

♥ Lottery tickets - for his birthday as many as his age.

♥ Massage gift certificate. Get a his and hers and go together.

♥ Trial membership to a gym.

♥ 6 months before his birthday, write one thing you admired, appreciated and loved about him each day. Buy a container in his favorite color and place each paper in it. Give this to him on his birthday.

♥ A book from the year he was born which lists everything that occurred that year.

♥ A jar of his favorite hot salsa with a note, "You make me soooo hot."

♥ A sexy pair of sunglasses.

♥ A squeezie stress ball.

♥ Colored golf balls.

♥ For wine lovers, a bottle of wine from the year he was born.

♥ Golf lessons.

♥ His favorite girl scout cookies (and he doesn't have to share.)

♥ Leather belt or wallet.

♥ License plate with your anniversary date.

♥ License plate with your birthday date.

♥ New computer game.

♥ New piece of sports equipment.

♥ Pen with his initials engraved.

♥ A big ribbon that says, # 1. Write after it whatever he's # 1 at in your heart.

♥ A calendar in his favorite theme. Write romantic notes on 2 days of every month.

♥ A garden stone with a romantic verse

♥ A plant with a big red bow.

♥ A year's membership in a beer or wine of the month club.

♥ Big screen tv.

♥ Bookends that are heart shaped.

♥ Books on his hobbies.

♥ Buy him subway tokens for one year.

♥ Car alarm.

♥ Chocolate cigars.

♥ Create a crossword puzzle with his favorite things such as sports teams, his buddies, his hobbies and your romantic history and dates.

♥ Cufflinks with both your initials.

♥ Dartboard.

♥ DVD of one season of his favorite show.

♥ For the fisherman, a plaque that says, "Best catch ever and his name." You can also write this on fancy paper and frame it.

♥ Framed certificate or diploma of his.

♥ Framed collectible of his (sports cards or signed baseball in a shadow box.)

♥ Get him an EZ pass for the turnpike.

♥ Get his friends, family and coworkers to write one thing they admire about him. Frame this.

♥ Gift certificate for music lessons.

♥ Gift certificate for 3 months of lawn care so he doesn't have to do it.

♥ Hand held massager.

♥ Heart shaped puzzle.

♥ If he's a teacher, get him a tie with apples on for the first day of school.

♥ Jewelry with diamonds.

♥ Laptop computer.

♥ Letter opener engraved with "I love you."

♥ Little black book with only your name and numbers. Fill the rest of the pages with romantic poems and reasons why you love him.

♥ Massage chair.

♥ Mini globe with a note that says, "You mean the world to me."

♥ Model kits of his favorite cars or airplanes.

♥ Monogrammed handkerchiefs with your initials.

♥ New boat.

♥ New car wrapped in a bow.

♥ New cell phone.

♥ New motorcycle.

♥ Pay his parking fee at work for 3 months.

♥ Silk tie.

♥ Satellite radio subscription.

♥ Something for his desk at work or something he can use at his job.

♥ Take his pet to be professionally photographed. Give him an 8" x 10" picture.

8 Romantic Ideas For Men

These romantic ideas for men will give you some great romance ideas and show you how to be romantic towards the woman in your life.

♥ Be her hero.

♥ Call her favorite radio station and dedicate a song to her.

♥ Call your home phone when you know she's not home and say, "I love you."

♥ Compliment her.

♥ Cook her Alphabet soup, spell "I love you" on the counter.

♥ Cut a heart out of construction paper. Write "I love you" and put it on her windshield.

♥ Get along with her family.

♥ Get along with her friends.

♥ Give her a back rub.

♥ Go shopping with her (pretend to enjoy it!). Surprise her with her favorite smoothie or pretzel at the mall food court.

♥ Go to the black Friday sale with her the day after Thanksgiving at 4 AM. Make a thermos of coffee for you both and bring the snack you prepared.

♥ Have a picture of her in your wallet.

♥ Help her fill up a basket full of goodies for a basket bingo.

♥ Hold doors open for her.

♥ If you're at home or in the car with the radio on, let her listen to her favorite station for a while.

♥ If you're on a trip without her, call her when you arrive and once per day until you return home.

♥ Keep her picture on your desk.

♥ Let her know if you'll be late.

♥ Listen to her tell you about her day.

♥ Make a flower out of paper.

♥ Put a love note in her coat pocket.

♥ Read Dear Abby and talk about it with her.

♥ Remember her birthday.

♥ Remember your anniversary.

♥ Save the last piece for her.

♥ Say you're sorry if you've done or said something to upset her.

♥ Send her a thank you card to thank her for her presence in your life.

♥ Send her love letters and poems.

♥ Send love text messages to her a few times a week. A simple "love you", "miss you" or "see you soon" is nice.

♥ Spontaneously take her hand and kiss it.

♥ Get a tissue. Write "I'm blown away by you." Leave it on the bathroom sink.

♥ If she's cold, offer her your coat.

♥ Put a note under her pillow that says, "You make my heart smile."

♥ Pencil her in on your work calendar. One hour for lunch or leave the office one hour early to be with her.

♥ Tell her she smells good.

♥ Tell her you had an amazing dream about her. Smile sexy as you say it.

♥ Treat her like a princess.

♥ When she's in the shower, put a towel in the dryer. Hand her the warm towel as she gets out.

♥ When you go out to eat, pull her chair out for her.

♥ When you're walking, to the car, to an event, at the mall or around the neighborhood, take her hand.

♥ Whistle as she walks by you.

♥ Wink at her.

♥ Write a song for her.

♥ Write "Joe loves Kathy" (whatever your names are!) in chalk on your driveway.

♥ Adore her.

♥ Brush her hair.

♥ Carry her through your front door.

♥ Change her car's oil.

♥ Cook on the grill for her.

♥ Do her taxes for her.

♥ Get her favorite bagel and cream cheese and bring it to her for breakfast.

♥ Get rid of your little black book once you are dating someone steadily.

♥ Get up first and make the coffee for a week.

♥ If she goes to the gym early in the morning, go with her. The same if she goes after work.

♥ Know her sizes.

♥ Lose the macho attitude with her.

♥ Make her a cup of tea. Attach a stickie love note that says, "you're hot."

♥ Paint her fingernails and toenails for her in your favorite color polish.

♥ Pick one day, and on that day every month, give her one flower.

♥ Put a love note in a book she's reading.

♥ Put a love note in her glove compartment.

♥ Put a rose on her pillow.

♥ Put a chocolate on her pillow.

♥ Reassure her if she's feeling unsure about something.

♥ Run your fingers through her hair.

♥ Spray a little of your cologne in her car.

♥ Sweep her off her feet.

♥ Turn down the bed for her.

♥ Write a romantic love letter in a foreign language for her. She'll have to translate it.

♥ Write, "I love you" on the bathroom mirror with your shaving cream.

♥ Always be a gentleman.

♥ Always treat her like the special lady that she is.

♥ Be her rock.

♥ Braid her hair for her.

♥ Call a department store in your town that sells men's and women's clothing and has a window on the street. Ask to have 2 mannequins put side by side in the window, one male and one female dressed. Make a sign for the male mannequin to hold that says, "(Your sweetie's name), will you marry me?"

♥ Call your local movie theater to see if you can put a "will you marry me?" message in the ads before the movie starts. One of the romantic proposal ideas she'll never forget!

♥ Don't go into debt trying to win her over.

♥ Give her a favorite shirt of yours so she can sleep in it.

♥ Give her a piggyback ride.

♥ Give her your shoulder to cry on.

♥ Have a magician make an engagement ring suddenly appear.

♥ Have flowers waiting in her hotel room when she goes out of town.

♥ If you're expecting, attend Lamaze classes together. Go with her for her doctor's appointments.

♥ Loosen up, don't be uptight.

♥ Mow, "I love you" in the grass.

♥ Put her number as the first one on your speed dial.

♥ Put love stamps on cards you mail to her.

♥ Remember, it's not always about you.

♥ Send her a romantic love letter via express delivery.

♥ Send a love letter via telegram.

♥ Send her an "I miss you" card when you won't see her for one day. Mail it so she gets it on the day you're not around.

♥ Tell her you would propose to her all over again if you could.

♥ Welcome her home by tying balloons to the fence or on the front door.

9 Romantic Things To Do For Men

Ideas for romantic things to do for the man in your life. Like women, men also appreciate romantic gestures and romantic words.

♥ Believe in him.

♥ Call his favorite radio station and dedicate a song to him.

♥ Carry a picture of him in your purse.

♥ Cheer his favorite sports team on by watching a game with him on tv occasionally.

♥ Do an errand for him he doesn't like to do himself.

♥ Don't try to change him.

♥ Go tailgating with him.

♥ Greet him at the door with nothing on.

♥ Hide a love note in his tool box.

♥ If he has to work late, take supper to him.

♥ If he's heading to the automotive, hardware or sporting goods store, go with him.

♥ Laugh at his jokes.

♥ Let him be your knight in shining armor.

♥ Let him channel surf.

♥ Let him fix something.

♥ Like his friends.

♥ Love and respect his family.

♥ Love his dog or cat as much as you love him.

♥ Place his picture in your office.

♥ Put a note on his windshield that says how much you appreciate him.

♥ Put love notes in his briefcase or jacket pocket.

♥ Read the sports page and learn about his favorite team.

♥ Recognize that he shows love through his actions as well as his words.

♥ Send him an email that only says "I love you."

♥ Tell him he smells good.

♥ Tell him he's terrific.

♥ The next time he's tinkering with his car, go tinker with him. Bring two glasses of his favorite cold drink - one for each of you.

♥ Try not to nag.

♥ Watch the Super Bowl with him every year. Root for who he's rooting for.

♥ Wear the perfume he bought you (or the sweater, the coat, the hat).

♥ Cheer him on throughout the years.

♥ Get some heart stickers at a craft store. Stick one on his steering wheel.

♥ Make him feel safe when he shares his feelings.

♥ Mess up his hair - lovingly.

♥ Put a love note in his cereal box.

♥ Put a note under his pillow that says, "You make me sooo happy".

♥ Seduce him.

♥ Spritz your perfume on a love note to him.

♥ When he's on his way home from work, meet him at the end of the driveway or block. Be happy to see him and shout "I missed you. I'm glad you're home."

♥ When the two of you are at the grocery store or doing a household chore together, look at him and say, "you're sooo sexy."

♥ Write a song for him.

♥ Write him a letter that says why you admire him.

♥ Write "I love you" in his Sports Illustrated magazine.

♥ Write "I love you" on a few of his golf balls.

♥ Crochet or knit something for him.

♥ Don't manipulate.

♥ Don't overanalyze everything he says.

♥ Fill a picnic basket with crackers, cheese, sandwiches, cold drinks and cookies and take it to his office for an indoor picnic.

♥ Help him gel his hair.

♥ Help him pick out an outfit for a special occasion or special meeting.

♥ Help him tie his tie.

♥ Make a fruit smoothie for him.

♥ Pinch him on the butt.

♥ Put a love note in the sports section of the newspaper.

♥ Put love notes in a cookie jar.

♥ Sew a button on for him.

♥ Buy him an angel food cake with a note that says, "You were definitely heaven sent".

♥ Don't man bash.

♥ Don't try and rush the relationship. Be patient and let it grow.

♥ Frame the romantic love poems or letters he writes you.

♥ Give him a break.

♥ Give him a chance.

♥ If he's out of town, call his cell phone in the morning for a wake up call.

♥ If you didn't take his advice, but should have, tell him, "you were right."

♥ If you like him, ask him out!

♥ Make him # 1 on your speed dial.

♥ Put heart stickers on cards you mail him.

♥ Put lipstick on. Kiss a sticky note and put it on his pillow.

♥ Put moisturizing lotion on his back.

♥ Say, "great job!" to him.

♥ Send a telegram with a romantic message.

♥ Send him a love letter via certified mail.

♥ Sit on his lap.

♥ Spray a little perfume in his car.

♥ Stick love notes on his work bench.

♥ Take the day off. Put on your sexy nightie. Call him at work, tell him what you're wearing and what you're thinking. Bet he comes home for lunch!

♥ Tell him he's the greatest.

♥ Try not to whine.

♥ Welcome him home by tying yellow ribbons to trees.

♥ When he's in the garage doing his man thing, take him some sandwiches, chips, his favorite drink and a blanket. Have a picnic right there.

♥ When he's out of town and staying at a hotel, call the desk and say something romantic for the message. Don't give a number!

♥ Write, "I love you" on the bathroom mirror with lipstick.

10 Romantic Birthday Ideas

These romantic birthday ideas let you and your soulmate celebrate the special day in the style you both love.

You'll find good date ideas, romance ideas and romantic tips for making your sweetie feel special.

Enjoy these ideas for a romantic birthday.

♥ A romantic fondue party for two. Feed chocolate covered strawberries to each other.

♥ Ad in the paper saying "Happy Birthday" and your sweetie's name.

♥ Bake her a homemade birthday cake on her birthday.

♥ Contact your local movie theater to see if they will give you and your sweetie a chance to see the newest romantic movie - just the two of you alone.

♥ Get a "Happy Birthday" banner at a party supply store. Attach it to the back of his or her car. Or sneak into their office before they get there and attach it to their desk.

♥ Make home made ice cream.

♥ Put "Happy Birthday" and your sweetie's name (and picture if you want!) on a billboard you rent.

♥ Put your sweetie's name on their local favorite restaurant's marquee to wish them a happy birthday on their special day. Take them to eat there.

♥ Rent a limo for a few hours. Prepare a picnic lunch with some cupcakes and champagne and party as you drive around town.

♥ Take an overnight trip to the casino. If your sweetie wins, let him or her keep the money without sharing.

♥ Take her out to eat where they will sing Happy Birthday to her.

♥ Take him to a place where they will sing Happy Birthday to him.

♥ Bake heart shaped cupcakes.

♥ Buy heart shaped candles for the cake.

♥ Buy her a tiara.

♥ Do a scavenger hunt.

♥ Get a card that you can record your own message.

♥ Get a caterer for a birthday dinner at home for the two of you. Get suggestions for romantic picnic food ideas.

♥ Get a pinata. Fill it with your sweetie's favorite candy, presents, and love letters.

♥ Get candles that don't blow out.

♥ Get her a corsage (like at prom time) to wear.

♥ Get party balloons at the dollar store. Slip love notes inside and blow them up.

♥ Get some silly string.

♥ Get two posters. Connect them together to form a big card. Write something romantic inside.

♥ Give your sweetie one cupcake with a heart shaped candle every day for the week of his or her birthday.

♥ Grab some chinese food, complete with your own personalized fortune cookies.

♥ Grab your camcorder and record yourself singing "Happy Birthday" to your sweetie. Show it to him or her.

♥ Have a gift delivered on the hour for 3 hours on your sweetie's birthday. Ideas: flowers, candy, balloons, fruit basket.

♥ Hire a sky writer to write "Happy Birthday (and your sweetie's name)".

♥ If you have earrings, a necklace or bracelet for your sweetie, put it in an empty medicine container. Ask if your sweetie would get you a refill then hand it to her.

♥ If you have a small gift, go to your sweetie's favorite fast food place. Order a .99c hamburger. Eat it. Wrap the gift in a napkin, then in the hamburger paper. Put it back in the bag and give this to your sweetie.

♥ Make a homemade birthday card from a piece of cardboard from a tv or computer box.

♥ On your birthday, give your sweetie a present.

♥ Order a heart shaped birthday cake.

♥ Send a singing telegram.

♥ Send romantic e-cards and romantic greeting cards.

♥ Send your sweetie's mother flowers on your sweetie's birthday.

♥ Throw a birthday party for your sweetie's pet.

♥ Throw confetti.

♥ Top the cake with edible flowers.

♥ Wear party hats and set off bottle rockets or sparklers.

♥ Wrap your sweetie's gift in the comics from the newspaper.

♥ Write "I love you" on the icing on the cake.

11 Romantic Dinner Ideas

These romantic dinner ideas offer you romantic picnic ideas and ideas for a romantic night.

If you're looking for food and dessert related romance ideas, you'll be able to find some ideas for the two of you here.

♥ Attend a pot luck dinner with his favorite dish.

♥ During the summer, go to a restaurant by the water and eat on the deck.

♥ Eat Chinese food together with chop sticks out of the same carton. Teach your sweetie how to use the chop sticks if he or she can't.

♥ Enjoy dinner at a sky top lounge as the sun sets.

♥ Find out which restaurants in your area have music playing. Request the pianist to play "your song" or the violinist to serenade your table.

♥ Get all dressed up, then go some place casual to eat.

♥ Get one ice cream cone or banana split and share it.

♥ Go camping, start a bonfire and cook her weenies and s'mores.

♥ Go grocery shopping together. Each buy one food your partner likes but you don't or haven't tried. Make it for your partner and eat your share.

♥ Go to a buffet restaurant and each fill the other's plate up. Give them something they don't normally get to eat so they can try it.

♥ Go to the airport and watch the airplanes taking off. If there's a restaurant there overlooking the landing strip, have dinner overlooking the runway.

♥ Go try Sushi. If your sweetie has never tried it, explain what each piece is and feed him or her.

♥ Have a picnic in the living room.

♥ Have a picnic under the stars in your backyard with your favorite beverage, cheese and grapes.

♥ Have a pot luck dinner for the two of you. Open cans, microwave frozen food and have a mix and match meal.

♥ Have a romantic meal at home surrounded by candlelight and your favorite fast food from the .99c menu.

♥ Host a backyard bbq at your place, charge a couple dollars admission and give the money to charity.

♥ In New York City, treat her to the famous Coney Island Hot Dogs. See the Statue of Liberty and Times Square.

♥ Make a date at your favorite restaurant once a month. Sit at the same booth or table and label it as "yours".

♥ Order dinner for your sweetie the next time you go out to eat.

♥ Order one milkshake with two straws.

♥ Take a romantic dinner cruise.

♥ Tour a winery. Have lunch there and do some wine sampling.

♥ While at your favorite tavern, order some wings, nachos and play romantic songs on the jukebox.

♥ Bake some heart shaped rolls.

♥ Buy heart shaped pasta.

♥ Buy some paper plates and plastic cups at the dollar store that have hearts on them.

♥ Cook dinner in the fireplace.

♥ Dine in your birthday suits.

♥ For dessert, bring out a plate with a note on that says, "I'm your dessert tonight".

♥ Get some party favors at the dollar store. Use them on the table at dinner.

♥ Put dimmer switches on the lights in your dining room.

♥ Serve her dinner in bed.

♥ Take turns blindfolding each other and feeding each other food such as grapes, cheese or chocolate.

♥ Tie ribbons around your wine glasses.

♥ Use your best dishes for your next meal. Dim the lights and dine in elegance.

12 Romantic Movies

Ahhh, romance movies. If you're looking for good date ideas or ideas for a romantic night, romantic movies and bubbly champagne drinks are a nice touch.

Romance stories come in lots of varieties, so couples can snuggle together and watch good chick flicks, romantic comedies or romantic thrillers.

Love movies offer cheap romantic ideas for couples counting pennies. Video rental stores often have 99 cent movie rentals if you rent more than one.

Pop up some popcorn, share your favorite alcoholic or non alcoholic drink and enjoy each other's company.

Winter date ideas feature movies, too. If it's snowing and blowing outside, scan the local tv paper listings to see when your sweetie's favorite romantic movie is playing.

Schedule an inside date with her to cuddle on the sofa and watch the movie. Give each other back rubs during the commercials.

If you're looking for Valentine's Day creative ideas or romantic birthday gift ideas, a few dvd's of your soulmate's classic romantic movies wrapped in his or her favorite color bow - along with a homemade card - score big points.

Make time to relax with your sweetheart watching your favorite couples movies and make memories to cherish in the future.

1930s Movies

A list of romantic 1930s movies for couples to watch together.

♥ A Farewell to Arms

♥ A Night at the Opera

♥ Algiers

♥ Alice Adams

♥ Anna Karenina

♥ Bringing Up Baby

♥ Camille

- ♥ Chained
- ♥ City Lights
- ♥ Cleopatra
- ♥ Dance Fools Dance
- ♥ Dark Victory
- ♥ Dodsworth
- ♥ Forsaking All Others
- ♥ Holiday
- ♥ It Happened One Night
- ♥ Jezebel
- ♥ King Kong
- ♥ Laughing Sinners
- ♥ Libeled Lady
- ♥ Love Affair
- ♥ Love Me Tonight
- ♥ Love on the Run
- ♥ Made For Each Other
- ♥ Maytime
- ♥ Midnight
- ♥ Morocco
- ♥ Mr. Deeds Goes to Town
- ♥ My Man Godfrey
- ♥ Ninotchka
- ♥ No Man of Her Own

♥ Of Human Bondage

♥ Platinum Blond

♥ Queen Christina

♥ Red Dust

♥ Red Headed Woman

♥ San Francisco

♥ Swing Time

♥ The Awful Truth

♥ The Hunchback of Notre Dame

♥ The Smiling Lieutenant

♥ The Possessed

♥ Top Hat

♥ Three Comrades

♥ Trouble in Paradise

♥ Wuthering Heights

1940s Movies

These 1940s movies are full of romance, drama and mystery. Cuddle together and pick one of these classics as "your movie".

♥ Adam's Rib

♥ All This and Heaven Too

♥ Anna and the King of Siam

♥ Brief Encounter

♥ Casablanca

♥ Christmas in July

- ♥ Dark Passage
- ♥ Double Indemnity
- ♥ Easter Parade
- ♥ For Whom the Bell Tolls
- ♥ Gone With The Wind
- ♥ Here Comes Mr Jordan
- ♥ His Girl Friday
- ♥ It's a Wonderful Life
- ♥ Jane Eyre
- ♥ Keeper of the Flame
- ♥ Key Largo
- ♥ Laura
- ♥ Letters From an Unknown Woman
- ♥ Love Letters
- ♥ Major Barbara
- ♥ Meet John Doe
- ♥ Mrs Miniver
- ♥ My Favorite Wife
- ♥ Notorious
- ♥ Now, Voyager
- ♥ Rebecca
- ♥ Random Harvest
- ♥ Strange Cargo
- ♥ That Hamilton Woman

- ♥ The Best Years of Our Lives
- ♥ The Big Sleep
- ♥ The Clock
- ♥ The Ghost and Mrs Muir
- ♥ The Heiress
- ♥ The Lady Eve
- ♥ The Lost Weekend
- ♥ The Man Who Came to Dinner
- ♥ The More the Merrier
- ♥ The Palm Beach Story
- ♥ The Philadelphia Story
- ♥ The Postman Always Rings Twice
- ♥ The Red Shoes
- ♥ The Sea of Grass
- ♥ The Shop Around the Corner
- ♥ To Have and Have Not
- ♥ Waterloo Bridge
- ♥ Without Love
- ♥ Woman of the Year

1950s Movies

Romantic '50s movies offer couples romance, suspense, comedy and drama.

- ♥ A Place in the Sun
- ♥ A Star is Born
- ♥ A Streetcar Named Desire

- ♥ A Summer Place
- ♥ All That Heaven Allows
- ♥ An Affair to Remember
- ♥ An American in Paris
- ♥ Desk Set
- ♥ Father of the Bride
- ♥ From Here to Eternity
- ♥ Gigi
- ♥ Guys and Dolls
- ♥ I'll Never Forget You
- ♥ It Happened to Jane
- ♥ Love is a Many Splendored Thing
- ♥ Love Me or Leave Me
- ♥ Marty
- ♥ Niagara
- ♥ On Moonlight Bay
- ♥ On the Waterfront
- ♥ Pat and Mike
- ♥ Picnic
- ♥ Pillow Talk
- ♥ Porgy and Bess
- ♥ Quiet Man
- ♥ Roman Holiday
- ♥ Sabrina

- ♥ Sayonara

- ♥ Singing in the Rain

- ♥ Some Like it Hot

- ♥ South Pacific

- ♥ Summertime

- ♥ Tammy and the Bachelor

- ♥ The African Queen

- ♥ The Bad and the Beautiful

- ♥ The Big Country

- ♥ The Bridges at Toko-Ri

- ♥ The Greatest Show on Earth

- ♥ The King and I

- ♥ The Lady and the Tramp

- ♥ The Last Time I Saw Paris

- ♥ The Tunnel of Love

- ♥ To Catch a Thief

- ♥ Three Coins in the Fountain

- ♥ Vertigo

- ♥ War and Peace

1960s Movies

1960s movies that couples can watch together on date nights or other special times.

- ♥ A Man and a Woman

- ♥ Barefoot in the Park

- ♥ Breakfast at Tiffany's
- ♥ Charade
- ♥ Cleopatra
- ♥ Doctor Zhivago
- ♥ Fanny
- ♥ Funny Girl
- ♥ Guess Who's Coming to Dinner
- ♥ Jules and Jim
- ♥ L'Avventura
- ♥ Lolita
- ♥ Love With the Proper Stranger
- ♥ Lover Come Back
- ♥ Mutiny on the Bounty
- ♥ My Fair Lady
- ♥ Please Don't Eat the Daisies
- ♥ Rachel, Rachel
- ♥ Romeo and Juliet
- ♥ Send Me No Flowers
- ♥ Splendor in the Grass
- ♥ Stolen Kisses
- ♥ The Apartment
- ♥ The Graduate
- ♥ The Sound of Music
- ♥ The Umbrellas of Cherbourg

♥ The Taming of the Shrew

♥ Two for the Road

♥ West Side Story

♥ Who's Afraid of Virginia Woolf?

1970s Movies

Choose one of the romantic '70s movies as "your movie" and celebrate your relationship and each other on your romantic movie night once a year on your anniversary.

♥ A Little Romance

♥ A Star is Born

♥ Alice Doesn't Live Here Anymore

♥ Annie Hall

♥ Bobby Deerfield

♥ California Suite

♥ Coming Home

♥ Grease

♥ Harold and Maude

♥ Head Over Heels

♥ High Pains Drifter

♥ Last Tango in Paris

♥ Love Story

♥ Manhattan

♥ Norma Rae

♥ Play Misty For Me

♥ Robin and Marian

- ♥ Rocky
- ♥ Ryan's Daughter
- ♥ Saturday Night Fever
- ♥ Same Time Next Year
- ♥ Shampoo
- ♥ Summer of '42
- ♥ Tess
- ♥ The Canterbury Tales
- ♥ The Chinese Connection
- ♥ The Goodbye Girl
- ♥ The Heartbreak Kid
- ♥ The Raging Moon
- ♥ The Way We Were
- ♥ The Virgin and the Gypsy
- ♥ Tim
- ♥ Time After Time

1980s Movies

'80s movies with comedy, drama, suspense and love.

- ♥ A Room With a View
- ♥ All the Right Moves
- ♥ Always
- ♥ American Gigolo
- ♥ An Officer and a Gentleman
- ♥ Atlantic City

- ♥ Baby, It's You
- ♥ Body Heat
- ♥ Bull Durham
- ♥ Dirty Dancing
- ♥ Flashdance
- ♥ Lady Jane
- ♥ Moonstruck
- ♥ My Beautiful Laundrette
- ♥ Nine 1/2 Weeks
- ♥ On Golden Pond
- ♥ Out of Africa
- ♥ Overboard
- ♥ Pretty in Pink
- ♥ Reds
- ♥ Romancing The Stone
- ♥ Roxanne
- ♥ Say Anything
- ♥ Sid & Nancy
- ♥ Sixteen Candles
- ♥ Something Wild
- ♥ Somewhere in Time
- ♥ Sophie's Choice
- ♥ Splash
- ♥ Terms of Endearment

♥ The Accidental Tourist

♥ The Fabulous Baker Boys

♥ The French Lieutenant's Woman

♥ The Last Metro

♥ The Princess Bride

♥ The Return of Martin Guerre

♥ The Thorn Birds

♥ The Unbearable Lightness of Being

♥ The Year of Living Dangerously

♥ Top Gun

♥ Twice in a Lifetime

♥ When Harry Met Sally

♥ Wings of Desire

♥ Witness

♥ Working Girl

1990s Movies

List of romantic '90s movies for couples.

♥ A Midsummer Night's Dream

♥ A Walk in the Clouds

♥ As Good As it Gets

♥ Beautiful Thing

♥ Beauty and the Beast

♥ Before Sunrise

♥ Braveheart

♥ Bridget Jones's Diary

♥ City of Angels

♥ Dances With Wolves

♥ Ever After

♥ Far and Away

♥ Forget Paris

♥ Ghost

♥ Hitch

♥ Hope Floats

♥ Jerry Maquire

♥ Jude

♥ Leaving Las Vegas

♥ Mrs. Brown

♥ My Best Friend's Wedding

♥ Notting Hill

♥ One Fine Day

♥ Only You

♥ Out of Sight

♥ Runaway Bride

♥ Rushmore

♥ Sense and Sensibility

♥ Shadowlands

♥ Shakespeare in Love

♥ Sleepless in Seattle

- ♥ Sliding Doors
- ♥ Strictly Ballroom
- ♥ The Age of Innocence
- ♥ The Bodyguard
- ♥ The Bridges of Madison County
- ♥ The Crying Game
- ♥ The Cutting Edge
- ♥ The English Patient
- ♥ The Horse Whisperer
- ♥ The Last of the Mohicans
- ♥ The Piano
- ♥ The Thomas Crowne Affair
- ♥ The Wedding Singer
- ♥ The Wings of the Dove
- ♥ Tin Cup
- ♥ Titanic
- ♥ Untamed Heart
- ♥ Up Close & Personal
- ♥ What Dreams May Come
- ♥ When a Man Loves a Woman
- ♥ While You Were Sleeping
- ♥ White Palace
- ♥ Wild at Heart
- ♥ You've Got Mail

Romantic Love Movies From the 2000's

- ♥ 40 Days and 40 Nights
- ♥ A Walk to Remember
- ♥ Alex and Emma
- ♥ Almost Famous
- ♥ Amelie
- ♥ Atonement
- ♥ Aurora Borealis
- ♥ Away From Her
- ♥ Bedazzled
- ♥ Before Sunset
- ♥ Chocolat
- ♥ Cold Mountain
- ♥ Definitely Maybe
- ♥ Down to You
- ♥ Elegy
- ♥ Hamlet
- ♥ Last Chance Harvey
- ♥ Lost in Translation
- ♥ Love and Basketball
- ♥ Love Actually
- ♥ Meet the Parents
- ♥ Moulin Rouge
- ♥ Mr. and Mrs. Smith

- ♥ Pearl Harbor

- ♥ Persuasion

- ♥ Pride and Prejudice

- ♥ Punch Drunk Love

- ♥ Restless

- ♥ Revolutionary Road

- ♥ Save the Last Dance

- ♥ Serendipity

- ♥ Shallow Hal

- ♥ Shrek

- ♥ Spanglish

- ♥ Stardust

- ♥ Swept Away

- ♥ The Curious Case of Benjamin Button

- ♥ The Jane Austen Book Club

- ♥ The Lake House

- ♥ The Last Kiss

- ♥ The Notebook

- ♥ The Phantom of the Opera

- ♥ The Princess Diaries

- ♥ The Rules of Attraction

- ♥ The Wedding Planner

- ♥ Waking Life

- ♥ Wall E

♥ Wedding Crashers

13 Ideas For A Romantic Night

These ideas for a romantic night give you and your sweetie romantic evening ideas to enjoy together.

Find adult romance ideas, bedroom ideas and romantic things to do.

Enjoy these romantic night ideas.

♥ Catch lightning bugs - then release them.

♥ Get a couple's massage.

♥ Get out the telescope and star gaze together.

♥ Go to a comedy club and laugh the night away.

♥ Go to a jazz club together.

♥ Go to the ballet, symphony or theatre and hold hands throughout the performance. Kiss during intermission.

♥ Go to the drive in movies and act like you're teenagers in love. Maybe watch the movie, too!

♥ Go to the local lover's lane and watch the sunset. Pack a sandwich or two.

♥ Go to the movie theatre, sit in the back and kiss during the movie.

♥ Have a movie night and watch your own home movies.

♥ Have a pajama party - just the two of you. Stay up all night watching movies, eating junk food, playing truth or dare and reminiscing.

♥ Hold hands and walk along the beach as the sun is going down. Watch the moon come up together.

♥ Horse drawn carriage ride.

♥ Make a fire and sit quietly together for an hour. Talk or just enjoy each other's company in the glow of the firelight.

♥ Name a star in your sweetie's name. Present the certificate to him or her in the glow of the moonlight.

♥ Once a month, watch a romantic movie at home together. Comedy, drama, thriller or chick flick!

♥ Pick one television show and make it "your show" and watch it together every week.

♥ Play board games together.

♥ Play card games together.

♥ Slow dance to a fast song.

♥ Slow dance to "your song".

♥ Soak your cares away together in a jacuzzi.

♥ Take a bubble bath together complete with champagne and candle light.

♥ Take a gondola ride.

♥ Take a shower together - use her shampoo and shower gel so you smell alike.

♥ Watch one reality show together. Each pick the player they think will win. If that player does win, the loser does something nice for the winner.

♥ Buy a massaging shower head and use it on each other.

♥ Buy a love seat for your patio for a romantic night under the stars and moon.

♥ Buy heart shaped lights. String them on your patio and keep them up all year.

♥ Check out the skyline in New York City at a top floor restaurant.

♥ Every time you have wine or champagne, make a special toast to each other.

♥ Get aromatherapy products to use.

♥ Head to the Eiffel Tower with the romantic glow of the lights.

♥ Rent some romantic foreign films to watch.

♥ See Niagara Falls.

♥ Try some aphrodisiacs.

14 Romantic Songs

Romantic songs are unique to each couple. Every couple should have an "our song" to call their own.

If you're looking for romance ideas or tips on how to be romantic, love songs need to be included.

The romantic words can take you back to your first date, the day you proposed, your wedding day or celebrating an anniversary.

As each song is special to each couple, different types of romantic music are unique to each relationship.

There's classic romance music from the '30s and '40s, folk romantic love songs from the '60s, love ballads from rock bands of the '80s, and modern romance movie songs from the '00s.

A love song can be sultry, sad, heartbreaking, uplifting and motivating. They speak of lost love, forbidden love, future love, hopeful love and "maybe we can try again" love.

If you want romantic evening ideas, play a cd filled with your romantic music, snuggle on the couch with champagne cocktails, toast to your love and let the memories come flooding back.

Cherish your soulmate and your relationship forever. Say "I love you" every day.

1930s Music

♥ All the Things You Are

♥ All Through The Night

♥ April in Paris

♥ At Long Last Love

♥ Body and Soul

♥ But Not For Me

♥ Cheek to Cheek

♥ Dream a Little Dream of Me

- ♥ East of the Sun
- ♥ Embraceable You
- ♥ Falling In Love With Love
- ♥ Heart and Soul
- ♥ How Deep is the Ocean
- ♥ I Don't Know Why
- ♥ I Get A Kick Out Of You
- ♥ In a Sentimental Mood
- ♥ Isn't It Romantic
- ♥ It's Easy to Remember
- ♥ I've Got My Love To Keep Me Warm
- ♥ I've Got You Under My Skin
- ♥ I've Told Ev'ry Little Star
- ♥ June in January
- ♥ Just One More Chance
- ♥ Let's Face the Music and Dance
- ♥ Love is Just Around The Corner
- ♥ Love Walked In
- ♥ Memories of You
- ♥ Moonglow My Ideal
- ♥ My Funny Valentine
- ♥ Night And Day
- ♥ Our Love Is Here To Stay
- ♥ PS I Love You

♥ Red Sails in the Sunset

♥ September Song

♥ Soft Lights and Sweet Music

♥ Smoke Gets in Your Eyes

♥ The Glory of Love

♥ The Lady's in Love With You

♥ The Song is You

♥ The Touch of Your Lips

♥ The Very Thought of You

♥ The Way You Look Tonight

♥ There's a Small Hotel

♥ What a Diff'rence a Day Made

♥ Where or When

♥ You Brought a New Kind of Love to Me

1940s Music

♥ A Little Bird Told Me

♥ All Through the Day

♥ Anniversary Song

♥ After All

♥ Be Careful, It's My Heart

♥ Buttons and Bows

♥ Come Rain Or Come Shine

♥ Day by Day

♥ Ev'ry Time We Say Goodbye

♥ Fools Rush In

♥ For Me and My Gal

♥ For You, For Me, For Evermore

♥ Forever and Ever

♥ Harbor Lights

♥ Have I Told You Lately That I Love You

♥ How Little We Know

♥ I Got It Bad And That Ain't Good

♥ I Wonder Who's Kissing Her Now

♥ I'll Be Seeing You

♥ I'm Beginning To See The Light

♥ I'm Making Believe

♥ It Only Happens When I Dance With You

♥ It's Been a Long, Long Time

♥ It's Magic

♥ I've Got My Eyes on You

♥ Laura

♥ Let There Be Love

♥ Linda

♥ Long Ago and Far Away

♥ Love Letters

♥ Love Like This Can't Last

♥ Love Somebody

♥ Moonlight Becomes You

♥ My Devotion

♥ My Foolish Heart

♥ My Heart Tells Me

♥ Oh! What it Seemed to Be

♥ Ole Buttermilk Sky

♥ Ring Around The Moon

♥ Sentimental Journey

♥ So In Love

♥ Some Enchanted Evening

♥ Stardust

♥ Sunday, Monday or Always

♥ That Old Black Magic

♥ The Anniversary Waltz

♥ The Nearness of You

♥ The Wonder Of You

♥ This Love of Mine

♥ To Each His Own

♥ Too Marvelous For Words

♥ You Can't Be True, Dear

♥ You Keep Coming Back Like A Song

♥ You'll Never Know

1950s Music

1950s music offers you some of the very best romantic music. Relax with your sweetie, put in a classic cd full of '50s music and go back in time with love.

♥ A Teenager in Love

♥ All at Once You Love Her

♥ All I Have to Do is Dream

♥ All of You

♥ All The Way

♥ And This is My Beloved

♥ Any Time

♥ Around the World

♥ As Long as I Live

♥ Autumn Leaves

♥ Band of Gold

♥ Chances Are

♥ Do I Love You Because You're Beautiful?

♥ Endlessly

♥ Fly Me to the Moon

♥ From Here to Eternity

♥ Goodnight My Love, Pleasant Dreams

♥ Half as Much

♥ Heartbreak Hotel

♥ Heartaches by the Number

♥ Hello, Young Lovers

♥ Hold My Hand

♥ I Can't Help It (If I'm Still in Love With You)

♥ I Have Dreamed

- ♥ I Left My Heart in San Francisco
- ♥ I Want You, I Need You, I Love You
- ♥ I Went to Your Wedding
- ♥ If You Were the Only Girl in the World
- ♥ I'll Be Home
- ♥ I've Grown Accustomed to Her Face
- ♥ Ivory Tower
- ♥ Just in Time
- ♥ Long Before I Knew You
- ♥ Love is a Simple Thing
- ♥ Love Letters in the Sand
- ♥ Love Makes the World Go Round
- ♥ Love Me Tender
- ♥ Loving You
- ♥ Magic Moments
- ♥ Memories are Made of This
- ♥ Misty
- ♥ Moments to Remember
- ♥ Mona Lisa
- ♥ My Happiness
- ♥ My Heart Cries For You
- ♥ My One and Only Love
- ♥ My Prayer
- ♥ My Special Angel

♥ Never Let Me Go

♥ Nevertheless (I'm in Love With You)

♥ No Other Love

♥ On the Street Where You Live

♥ Once Upon a Dream

♥ Only You (and You Alone)

♥ Puppy Love

♥ Put Your Head on My Shoulder

♥ Sea of Love

♥ Smoke Gets in Your Eyes

♥ Stranger in Paradise

♥ Take Me to Your Heart Again

♥ Teach Me Tonight

♥ Tears on My Pillow

♥ That's Amore

♥ The Twelfth of Never

♥ The Wonder of You

♥ Three Coins in the Fountain

♥ Till We Two Are One

♥ To Love Again

♥ True Love

♥ Twilight Time

♥ Unchained Melody

♥ Unforgettable

- ♥ When I Fall in Love
- ♥ Why
- ♥ Wish You Were Here
- ♥ With All My Heart
- ♥ You Are Beautiful
- ♥ You Belong to Me
- ♥ You Don't Know Me
- ♥ Young at Heart
- ♥ Young Love

1960s Music

- ♥ A Time For Us
- ♥ All My Loving
- ♥ All You Need is Love
- ♥ And I Love Her
- ♥ Beginnings
- ♥ Bus Stop
- ♥ Can't Help Falling in Love
- ♥ Cherish
- ♥ Dedicated to the One I Love
- ♥ For Once in My Life
- ♥ Goin' Out of My Head
- ♥ Happy Together
- ♥ Hold Me, Thrill Me, Kiss Me
- ♥ Hooked on a Feeling

♥ How Can I Be Sure

♥ How Sweet It Is (to be loved by you)

♥ I Can't Stop Loving You

♥ I Got You Babe

♥ I Think We're Alone Now

♥ I Was Made to Love Her

♥ I Will Follow Him

♥ I Will Wait For You

♥ I Wish You Love

♥ If Ever I Would Leave You

♥ I'm Sorry

♥ I'm Your Puppet

♥ Leaving On a Jet Plane

♥ Let It Be Me

♥ Love (Can Make You Happy)

♥ Michelle

♥ Midnight Confessions

♥ Moon River

♥ More Today Than Yesterday

♥ My Cherie Amour

♥ My Cup Runneth Over

♥ My Love

♥ My World Is Empty Without You

♥ Ooo Baby Baby

♥ Our Day Will Come

♥ Puppy Love

♥ Raindrops

♥ Rhythm of the Rain

♥ Save The Last Dance For Me

♥ Sealed With A Kiss

♥ Silence is Golden

♥ Somewhere My Love

♥ Starting Here, Starting Now

♥ Strangers in the Night

♥ Take Good Care Of My Baby

♥ Teen Angel

♥ Tell It Like It Is

♥ The Look of Love

♥ The Rain, The Park And Other Things

♥ The Sun Ain't Gonna Shine Anymore

♥ The Tracks of My Tears

♥ Then You Can Tell Me Goodbye

♥ This Guy's in Love With You

♥ This Magic Moment

♥ Traces

♥ Unchained Melody

♥ You're My Soul and Inspiration

♥ You've Lost That Lovin' Feeling

♥ When a Man Loves a Woman

♥ Where Did Our Love Go

♥ Will You Still Love Me Tomorrow

♥ Worst That Could Happen

♥ You Don't Have to Say You Love Me

♥ You Were on My Mind

♥ You've Lost That Lovin' Feeling

1970s Music

♥ After the Love Has Gone

♥ After the Lovin'

♥ Afternoon Delight

♥ All I Know

♥ Alone Again (Naturally)

♥ Annie's Song

♥ Babe

♥ Baby Come Back

♥ Baby I'm a Want You

♥ Best Thing That Ever Happened to Me

♥ Betcha By Golly, Wow

♥ Bluer Than Blue

♥ Can't Fight This Feeling

♥ Close to You

♥ Don't Give Up on Us

♥ Even The Nights Are Better

- ♥ Everything I Own

- ♥ Feelings

- ♥ Fooled Around And Fell In Love

- ♥ For the Good Times

- ♥ Have I Told You Lately

- ♥ He Don't Love You (Like I Love You)

- ♥ How Deep Is Your Love

- ♥ How Much I Feel

- ♥ (Last Night) I Didn't Get to Sleep at All

- ♥ I Go Crazy

- ♥ I Honestly Love You

- ♥ I Just Can't Help Believing

- ♥ I Just Fall in Love Again

- ♥ I Like Dreamin'

- ♥ I Need You

- ♥ I'd Love You to Want Me

- ♥ I'd Really Love To See You Tonight

- ♥ If

- ♥ If You Leave Me Now

- ♥ I'll Always Love You

- ♥ I'll Never Love This Way Again

- ♥ I'm Not In Love

- ♥ Into The Night

- ♥ It's Impossible

- ♥ Just When I Needed You Most
- ♥ Just Remember I Love You
- ♥ Just You 'N' Me
- ♥ Key Largo
- ♥ Lady (by Styx)
- ♥ Last Song
- ♥ Laughter In The Rain
- ♥ Lead Me On
- ♥ Longer
- ♥ Lost In Love
- ♥ Love is in the Air
- ♥ Love Story (Where Do I Begin)
- ♥ Love Will Keep Us Together
- ♥ Lovin' You
- ♥ Make It With You
- ♥ Maybe I'm Amazed
- ♥ More Than a Feeling
- ♥ My Eyes Adored You
- ♥ My Love
- ♥ Never Be The Same
- ♥ Nobody Does It Better
- ♥ One In A Million You
- ♥ One Less Bell to Answer
- ♥ One More Night

- ♥ Please Come To Boston
- ♥ Precious and Few
- ♥ Reunited
- ♥ Right Here Waiting
- ♥ Right Time of the Night
- ♥ Rosanna
- ♥ Sad Eyes
- ♥ Sara
- ♥ She Believes in Me
- ♥ She's a Lady
- ♥ She's Gone
- ♥ Show and Tell
- ♥ Somewhere Out There
- ♥ Stuck On You
- ♥ Sunshine on My Shoulders
- ♥ Superstar
- ♥ The Air That I Breathe
- ♥ The First Time Ever I Saw Your Face
- ♥ The Most Beautiful Girl
- ♥ The Things We Do For Love
- ♥ Theme from Mahogany (Do You Know Where You're Going To)
- ♥ Touch me in the Morning
- ♥ Three Times a Lady
- ♥ Time In A Bottle

- ♥ Unforgettable
- ♥ We're All Alone
- ♥ We've Only Just Begun
- ♥ When A Man Loves A Woman
- ♥ You Are Everything
- ♥ You Are So Beautiful
- ♥ You Are The Woman
- ♥ You Light Up My Life
- ♥ You Make Me Feel Brand New
- ♥ You Needed Me
- ♥ Your Song
- ♥ You're The Inspiration
- ♥ You're The Only Woman

1980s Music

- ♥ A Groovy Kind of Love
- ♥ Against All Odds
- ♥ All Cried Out
- ♥ All Out of Love
- ♥ Almost Paradise
- ♥ Alone
- ♥ Always
- ♥ Always on My Mind
- ♥ Amanda
- ♥ Angel of the Morning

- ♥ Because I Love You
- ♥ Blue Eyes
- ♥ Can't Fight This Feeling
- ♥ Careless Whisper
- ♥ Could've Been
- ♥ Crazy For You
- ♥ Crying
- ♥ Do That To Me One More Time
- ♥ Don't Know Much
- ♥ Don't Walk Away
- ♥ Endless Love
- ♥ Eternal Flame
- ♥ Faithfully
- ♥ Forever (by Kiss)
- ♥ Glory of Love
- ♥ Greatest Love Of All
- ♥ Heartbreaker
- ♥ Hello
- ♥ Here And Now
- ♥ I Guess That's Why They Call It the Blues
- ♥ I Just Called To Say I Love You
- ♥ I Knew You Were Waiting (For Me)
- ♥ I Need Love
- ♥ I Want To Know What Love Is

♥ I Would Die 4 U

♥ If I Could

♥ I'll Be There For You

♥ I'll Never Let You Go (Angel Eyes)

♥ It Must Have Been Love

♥ Keep on Loving You

♥ Lady in Red

♥ Love of a Lifetime

♥ Never Tear Us Apart

♥ Nothing's Gonna Change My Love For You

♥ Oh Sherrie

♥ One More Night

♥ Open Arms

♥ Say You, Say Me

♥ Sea of Love

♥ Stop to Love

♥ Suddenly

♥ Take My Breath Away

♥ The One That You Love

♥ The Rose

♥ The Search is Over

♥ Tonight I Celebrate My Love

♥ Total Eclipse of the Heart

♥ True

♥ Truly

♥ Up Where We Belong

♥ You've Really Got a Hold on Me

♥ Waiting For A Girl Like You

♥ When I Look Into Your Eyes

♥ When I See You Smile

♥ When I'm With You

♥ With You I'm Born Again

♥ Woman In Love

'90s Music

♥ 2 Become 1

♥ A Whole New World

♥ All I Have to Give

♥ All I Wanna Do is Make Love to You

♥ All My Life

♥ Always

♥ Anything

♥ As Long As You Love Me

♥ Beautiful in My Eyes

♥ Because I Love You

♥ Because You Loved Me

♥ Breathe Again

♥ Building A Mystery

♥ Cherish

♥ Come What May

♥ Cry

♥ Don't Let Go (Love)

♥ Dreams

♥ Easy

♥ End of the Road

♥ Even When I'm Sleeping

♥ Everybody Hurts

♥ (Everything I Do) I Do It For You

♥ Fields of Gold

♥ Finally Found

♥ Foolish Games

♥ From This Moment

♥ Hard to Say I'm Sorry

♥ Have I Told You Lately

♥ Have You Ever Really Loved a Woman

♥ Hold On

♥ How Am I Supposed to Live

♥ How Can We Be Lovers

♥ How Come How Long

♥ How Do I Live

♥ I Can't Make You Love Me

♥ I Don't Want to Miss a Thing

♥ I Swear

- ♥ I Want It That Way
- ♥ I Will Always Love You
- ♥ I Will Come to You
- ♥ I Won't Let You Down
- ♥ I'll Make Love To You
- ♥ I'll Stand By You
- ♥ It's Alright
- ♥ Kiss From a Rose
- ♥ Last Night
- ♥ Love is All Around
- ♥ Love That Will Be Done
- ♥ Lullaby
- ♥ More Than Words
- ♥ My Heart Will Go On
- ♥ Never Ever
- ♥ Nothing Compares to You
- ♥ One Sweet Day
- ♥ Please Forgive Me
- ♥ Save the Best For Last
- ♥ Say it Once
- ♥ Secret Garden
- ♥ Something About the Way You Look Tonight
- ♥ Sometimes
- ♥ Sometimes Love Just Ain't Enough

- ♥ Stay
- ♥ Stay Another Day
- ♥ Thank You
- ♥ That's The Way Love Goes
- ♥ The Power of Love
- ♥ To Make You Feel My Love
- ♥ Truly Madly Deeply
- ♥ Unbreak My Heart
- ♥ Until the Time is Through
- ♥ What Comes Naturally
- ♥ Would I Lie to You
- ♥ You Were Meant For Me
- ♥ You're Still the One

Romantic Love Songs From the 2000's

- ♥ A New Day Has Come
- ♥ Again and Again
- ♥ All About Lovin' You
- ♥ All You Wanted
- ♥ Almost Here
- ♥ Amazed
- ♥ Angel Eyes
- ♥ Angels
- ♥ Because of You
- ♥ Be Without You

- ♥ Boy (I Need You)
- ♥ Brand New Day
- ♥ Breathe
- ♥ Breathe in Now
- ♥ By Your Side
- ♥ Come Away With Me
- ♥ Come Back to Me
- ♥ Could I Have This Kiss Forever
- ♥ Cruisin
- ♥ Everything
- ♥ Fallin'
- ♥ Heartbeats
- ♥ Heavy on My Heart
- ♥ Hero
- ♥ Hurt
- ♥ Hurts So Bad
- ♥ I Believe
- ♥ I Lay My Love on You
- ♥ I Still...
- ♥ I Wanna Be With You
- ♥ I Wanna Love You Forever
- ♥ I Want Love
- ♥ If Tomorrow Never Comes
- ♥ Just Want to Know

- ♥ Live For Love
- ♥ Love Love Love
- ♥ Love 2 Love
- ♥ More Than That
- ♥ Never the Same Again
- ♥ Nobody Wants to Be Lonely
- ♥ One Day in Your Life
- ♥ Only You
- ♥ Out of the Blue
- ♥ Real Love
- ♥ Rise & Fall
- ♥ Running
- ♥ Shadow
- ♥ She Believes in Me
- ♥ She Will Be Loved
- ♥ Signed, Sealed, Delivered I'm Yours
- ♥ Something About You
- ♥ Songbird
- ♥ Take My Breath Away
- ♥ Thank You For Loving Me
- ♥ The Hardest Part
- ♥ The Long Goodbye
- ♥ The One I Love
- ♥ The Way You Love Me

- ♥ This I Promise You

- ♥ Together We Are One

- ♥ Touch

- ♥ Unchained Melody

- ♥ Walk on By

- ♥ Watch Over Me

- ♥ We Belong Together

- ♥ We've Got Tonight

- ♥ What's Left of Me

- ♥ When You Kiss Me

- ♥ When You Say You Love Me

- ♥ World Filled With Love

- ♥ You and Me

- ♥ You Raise Me Up

- ♥ You'll Be In My Heart

15 Romantic Surprise Ideas

These romantic surprise ideas include ideas for a fun date, cheap romantic ideas, and free romance ideas.

♥ Ask him out on a romantic date that you plan. Keep it a surprise until you get there.

♥ Don't write "wash me" on her dirty car, write "I love you".

♥ Email her a line of poetry once a week.

♥ Find out where his favorite sports team practices. Tell him you'll treat him to dinner, then drive to where the practice is.

♥ Get her favorite love song on CD. Take her to dinner one evening. On the way home, pull over somewhere private, put the CD in, get out of the car and ask her to slow dance as the sun sets.

♥ Go to a flea market and purchase an inexpensive item you think she would like. Romantic surprise ideas don't have to be expensive!

♥ Have a surprise date by going to the restaurant section in your phone book. One person closes their eyes and puts their finger down. Where it lands is where you will go eat.

♥ Hide Hershey's Kisses in her make up bag.

♥ Hide Hershey's Kisses in his brief case.

♥ Hop in the car, and without plans, drive for a preset amount of time. When the time is up, see what's around - grab a coffee, get some ice cream and make this "your place" to go at least a few times a year.

♥ If she always cooks, surprise her with dinner one night. Order it, cook it or take her out!

♥ Make a mess on the counter by spelling out "I love you" with mustard or ketchup in squeeze bottles.

♥ Make her breakfast in bed.

♥ Once a week, use stickie notes and say something romantic to your partner. Put them on the refrigerator, in his brief case, on the bathroom mirror, on the bed.

♥ Plan a romantic date for her by leaving cryptic notes as to where to meet you - "drive 4.5 miles, turn left, go another 2.4 miles, and I'll be waiting on the sidewalk for you."

♥ Send romantic e-cards a few times a year to your sweetie.

♥ Send romantic greeting cards via snail mail a few times a year - not on a special occasion but just because you're thinking of your sweetie.

♥ Surprise her by cleaning the house or doing laundry.

♥ Snail mail her a party invitation - where it will be only the two of you going out to your favorite spot.

♥ Stop at a bake sale and purchase your sweetie's favorite treat.

♥ Surprise her by stopping by her office and whisking her off to lunch.

♥ Surprise her with flowers occasionally.

♥ Surprise him by whisking him off to his favorite lunch spot.

♥ Surprise him with flowers occasionally.

♥ Take her for a motorcycle ride. Pull over at the park and surprise her with sandwiches, chips and a drink you packed.

♥ Tell her you'll take care of dinner. Stop for some chicken or chinese food on your way home from work. Put a blanket on your front porch or balcony and have a picnic, just the two of you.

♥ Text her just to say "hi".

♥ Wash her car for no reason.

♥ Wash his car for no reason.

♥ Browse the newspaper and magazines for romantic travel destinations. Note what your sweetie likes and plan surprise weekend romantic vacations.

♥ Call his buddies and invite them over Friday or Saturday night. Order pizza, have snacks ready. Don't tell your sweetie until his friends arrive. Then leave and go out with your girlfriends while the guys have fun.

♥ Establish a college scholarship at your sweetie's alma mater.

♥ Gather his fraternity brothers or her sorority sisters together for a surprise evening.

♥ Get a massage therapist to come to your home one evening or weekend.

♥ Get the snow and ice off her car. Start her car so it's warm when she leaves.

♥ Give your sweetie a small gift the month before and the month after his or her birthday on the date of his birthday.

♥ Go to your sweetie's office when you know they will be out. Hide their favorite snack foods or beverage in their drawer.

♥ Guys, tell her you won't be able to see her because the big game is on. Record the game, then surprise her by stopping by to take her out for dinner. You can watch the game when you get back home.

♥ Hide some flowers in the dishwasher. Ask her to help you unload it.

♥ If a new flower shop opens, take her there after work but don't tell her where you're going. Let her pick out a bouquet.

♥ If a new store opens in your city, surprise your sweetie by taking him or her there. Let your love pick up a trinket, no matter what kind of store it is! Have some fun with it!

♥ If your sweetie is out of town and you're supposed to pick them up at the airport, call and say something came up and you won't be there until the next morning (or later that day). Tell them to go to a nearby hotel where you reserved a room. You'll be waiting at the door when they arrive.

♥ If your sweetie gets a promotion, buy a small gift or take them out for a nice dinner.

♥ If your sweetie likes tomatos, plant a tomato plant.

♥ If your sweetie is going on a trip, head to a discount store and pick up lots of travel size shampoos, lotions, hairsprays, mouthwash and toothpaste. Present it to him or her in a nice traveling cosmetic case.

♥ Pay your sweetie's parking ticket for him or her.

♥ Put a menu from a restaurant under his wiper blade. Tell him to meet you there at a certain time.

♥ Romantic anniversary ideas - put "Happy Anniversary" (and your sweetie's name) in an ad on the back page of the newspaper on your special day.

♥ Take your sweetie out for a surprise dinner in October on Sweetest Day.

♥ Tell your sweetie you have to work late. Show up at their place of work and whisk them off to a romantic dinner.

♥ Think of a restaurant where your sweetie loves the dessert. Pick him or her up, and stop at a favorite restaurant of your love's for a drink. Then head off to another of their favorite restaurants for dinner. Finally, head to the third restaurant for dessert.

♥ Throw small stones at her bedroom window. When she looks out, get down on one knee and sing.

♥ Wrap up a book on the city you have chosen as a surprise romantic getaway. Put in a note saying to pack because you're leaving in a few hours.

16 Romantic Tips

Romantic tips for a healthy and happy relationship.

Couples need romantic words and romantic gestures to sustain a mutually satisfying relationship.

♥ Always make time to listen to each other.

♥ Be friends as well as lovers.

♥ Be patient with each other.

♥ Be selfless not selfish.

♥ Brag about each other.

♥ Compromise.

♥ Do what your sweetie wants every other month, whether you want to or not.

♥ Don't judge each other.

♥ Focus on each other's strengths, not weaknesses.

♥ Grow together over the years and not apart.

♥ Honor your wedding vows every day.

♥ Hug each other once per day.

♥ If the lights go out during a storm, head to bed.

♥ Kiss hello and goodbye once a day.

♥ Let her have her girls nights out.

♥ Let him have his guys nights out.

♥ Make each other a priority in your lives.

♥ Never be afraid to apologize.

♥ Never go to bed angry.

♥ Never say things you would regret later. Count to ten or bite your tongue.

♥ Never take each other for granted.

♥ Once a month give your sweetie a few hours to do whatever they want. Sleep, spend it with friends, it's their call.

♥ Point out rainbows to your sweetie.

♥ Respect each other.

♥ Say "I love you" every day.

♥ Say one nice thing to your partner each day.

♥ Say "please" and "thank you."

♥ See the good in each other.

♥ Stand by each other.

♥ Avoid behaviors that turn your partner off.

♥ Be flexible.

♥ Be kind to each other.

♥ Cherish each other.

♥ Do more of the behaviors that turn your partner on.

♥ Empathize with each other.

♥ Love unconditionally.

♥ Practice virtue, live your morals and values.

♥ Remember that noone and no relationship is perfect.

♥ Sacrifice for each other.

♥ Support each other.

♥ Treasure each other.

♥ Trust each other.

♥ Work on having open communication.

♥ Always wear your wedding rings.

♥ Be accepting of each other.

♥ Be attentive to each other.

♥ Be devoted to each other.

♥ Be intimate with each other - emotional as well as physical.

♥ Be loyal to each other.

♥ Be strong to each other.

♥ Be thoughtful.

♥ Every year celebrate the date of your first date, first kiss, day you got engaged and your wedding day.

♥ Comfort each other.

♥ Connect with each other.

♥ Consult with each other.

♥ Control jealous feelings.

♥ Don't argue about money. Work on a budget and the checkbook together.

♥ Don't be critical.

♥ Don't be stubborn.

♥ Don't criticize.

♥ Don't fight in public.

♥ Don't give each other the silent treatment.

♥ Don't hold a grudge.

♥ Don't snoop through each other's things.

♥ Don't sulk.

♥ Embrace change together.

♥ Encourage each other.

♥ Give and take.

♥ Give each other courage.

♥ Give each other hope.

♥ Give each other the benefit of the doubt.

♥ Give each other the gift of time. It doesn't matter what you do, just spend some alone time together each day.

♥ Go out of your way for each other.

♥ If a problem arises, work on resolving it together quickly.

♥ Keep promises to each other.

♥ Never get lazy in your relationship.

♥ Never insult each other.

♥ Only flirt with each other.

♥ Say what your heart feels.

♥ Share household chores.

♥ Share the good and the bad with each other.

♥ Share what's on your mind.

♥ Touch each other.

♥ Value each other's uniqueness.

♥ Agree to disagree at times.

♥ Be able to forget.

♥ Be able to forgive.

♥ Be polite.

♥ Care about each other.

- ♥ Cheer each other on.

- ♥ Court each other all the years of your relationship.

- ♥ Don't be complacent.

- ♥ Don't complain.

- ♥ Don't nitpick.

- ♥ Don't yell at each other.

- ♥ Double date with other happy couples.

- ♥ Don't name call.

- ♥ Don't treat each other like children.

- ♥ Inspire each other.

- ♥ Keep things in perspective.

- ♥ Learn how to negotiate.

- ♥ Look together towards the future.

- ♥ Motivate each other.

- ♥ Stay committed to each other and your relationship.

- ♥ Take steps to change a problem or behavior before it gets out of hand.

- ♥ The past is the past. Let it go.

17 Spiritual Romance Ideas

These romance ideas allow couples to grow spiritually together.

When we think of romantic presents, we often think of gifts we can open. But these also include gifting of ourselves to others.

Romantic things to do sometimes involve opening our hearts to other people.

♥ Attend Eucharistic Adoration together.

♥ Attend Good Friday services together.

♥ Attend Holy Thursday services together.

♥ Attend the Easter Vigil together.

♥ Be examples of faith to each other on your spiritual journeys.

♥ Be mentors to a young couple who are getting ready to be married.

♥ During Lent, attend Stations of the Cross together.

♥ Go on a pilgrimage together.

♥ Go on a spiritual retreat together.

♥ If your church recites the "Our Father", hold hands while saying it.

♥ Join a spiritual book club together.

♥ Join your church choir together.

♥ Kiss during the sign of peace.

♥ Love your spouse as much as you love God and see God in your spouse.

♥ Mark your favorite bible passages about love and read these together.

♥ Mentor someone who has fallen away from the church together.

♥ Offer to drive a parishioner without a car to church each week together.

♥ Offer to write a column together for your church bulletin on how to have a holy marriage.

♥ Pick a favorite saint together and pray to them.

♥ Pick out one religious item together and place it in your home.

♥ Pray for each other daily.

♥ Pray the rosary together.

♥ Pray together.

♥ Read the bible together.

♥ Read Theology of the Body together.

♥ Take a religious class together.

♥ Visit a shrine together.

♥ Volunteer together at a soup kitchen.

♥ Volunteer together at church.

♥ Do some contemplative reading together.

♥ Give each other hope.

♥ Give each other peace.

♥ Give each other tranquility.

♥ Go to Lourdes.

♥ Go to Jerusalem.

♥ Head to Rome. Make sure to see the Vatican.

♥ Journal together.

♥ Make a collage out of sayings in the bible that contain the word "love".

♥ Meditate together.

♥ Neatly write the words down to your favorite hymn. Frame it and hang it up.

♥ Read a book on soulmates together.

♥ Renew your wedding vows.

- ♥ Tour historic churches.

- ♥ Visit a monastery.

- ♥ At a specific time each day during the work week, stop and say a prayer of thanksgiving that you have your sweetie.

- ♥ Attend confession together at least twice per year.

- ♥ Frame a copy of traditional wedding vows and hang up in your home.

- ♥ Get a picture or painting of the church you got married in. Frame it and hang it up.

- ♥ Give your soulmate prayer cards specific to their situation.

- ♥ Join Cursillo.

- ♥ Love each other unconditionally.

- ♥ Men, become a deacon. Women, stand by and support him on it.

- ♥ Remember, your soulmate is a gift from God.

- ♥ See your spouse through God's eyes.

- ♥ Send your sweetie a prayer book in time of need.

- ♥ Share a hymnal at church.

- ♥ Tape inspirational messages to the refrigerator.

- ♥ When your sweetie sneezes, say "Bless you."

18 Romantic Valentine Ideas

These romantic Valentine ideas offer you and your sweetie unique ideas for Valentines Day, date ideas and gift ideas.

♥ Buy her favorite movie on DVD for Valentine's Day.

♥ Buy his favorite movie on DVD for Valentine's Day.

♥ Order a bag of M&M's that can be personalized with a special phrase or an "I love you".

♥ Make a cd of your sweetie's favorite songs. If you sing, record yourself singing the songs.

♥ Make a slideshow of your life together on the computer with photos you've taken over the years.

♥ Make chocolate covered strawberries together then feed them to each other.

♥ Play the card game Hearts on Valentine's Day.

♥ Save ticket stubs, napkins, receipts or match books from places you went and things you did for one year. Put them in a scrapbook and give them to her.

♥ Use the cardboard on back of a notepad. Write a romantic message to your sweetie and what you plan to do with him or her on February 14th. Cut it into different shapes. Mail it along with your card to your honey. When they open the card they will need to assemble the puzzle to find out what the romantic plans are.

♥ Write her a love letter for Valentine's Day. Read it to her.

♥ Write her a romantic poem and give it to her on Valentine's Day.

♥ Write him a love letter for Valentine's Day. Read it to him.

♥ Bake a heart shaped cake.

♥ Bake heart shaped cookies together.

♥ Buy a small box of heart shaped candy. Write your special love message on the inside of the lid.

♥ Buy a heart shaped jacuzzi together. Use it often.

♥ Get red heart shaped confetti for the bath tub. Take a bath together.

♥ Guys, dress up like Cupid and tell her she has your heart forever.

♥ Have your picture taken side by side on the large cut outs where only your heads are showing.

♥ Head to the Poconos and a room with a heart shaped tub.

♥ Propose.

♥ Put an ad on the back page of your local newspaper for February 14th that says "Jim S. loves Sue S." Or put your full names in.

♥ Put one rose on her windshield before she goes to work.

♥ Say happy V day to your sweetie on a local tv station's free public service or paid advertisement.

♥ Sprinkle red confetti on your sweetie's car.

♥ Tie a red balloon to his car in the morning before he leaves.

♥ Bake a heart shaped pie.

♥ Celebrate for 2 days in a row.

♥ Draw hearts on the bathroom mirror with lipstick.

♥ Eat on the heart shaped plates.

♥ Fill up the heart shaped ice cube trays.

♥ For the month of February, put linens and pillow cases with hearts on the bed.

♥ Get a blow up Cupid for a decoration.

♥ Get out the heart shaped place mats.

♥ Get out the heart shaped soaps on a string.

♥ Go back to the hotel you stayed at on your honeymoon.

♥ Hang a heart shaped wreath on the door.

♥ Have heart shaped pancakes for breakfast.

♥ Head to a honeymoon suite.

♥ Make a pizza in a heart shape.

♥ Make a wreath by gluing together red gum drops.

♥ Make heart shapes out of red licorice.

♥ Make red ice cubes by putting some food coloring in the water before you freeze it.

♥ Make smores in the fireplace.

♥ Order a cookie bouquet wrapped in a red bow.

♥ Plan a romance party with your friends. Have each couple bring one romantic exchange gift.

♥ Put up the red Christmas lights for the week.

♥ Red silk tie and boxers for him.

♥ Share red jelly beans.

♥ The day after, February 15th, stock up on gift bags and other items on sale. Give to your sweetie throughout the year.

♥ Tie with hearts.

♥ Try to find red or pink lightbulbs.

19 U.S. Romantic Travel Destinations

These romantic travel destinations offer couples spots for romantic proposals, romantic vacations and weekend getaways.

If you're looking for romantic places in your city, a quick one day getaway, a romantic picnic spot or scenic outlook to watch a sunset, these attractions in all 50 states will allow you to find your perfect location.

Are you and your sweetie looking for ideas for a fun date? These activities include fun night date ideas and inexpensive romantic ideas.

Romance is all about attitude and being with the person you love. It's a state of mind, and each couple will have their own ideas of which places and activities they find romantic.

From state parks to amusement parks to scenic overlooks, any place is romantic when you're sharing it with your soulmate.

Romantic Things To Do In Alabama

Fun, romantic things to do in Alabama for couples. Visit Alabama attractions, some offering cheap date ideas. Enjoy fun and romance with your love.

- ♥ Alabama Fan Club And Museum

- ♥ Alabama Jazz Hall of Fame

- ♥ Alabama Point on the Gulf Shores

- ♥ Alabama Shakespeare Festival

- ♥ Barber Vintage Motorsports Museum, Leeds

- ♥ Bellingrath Gardens and Home

- ♥ Birmingham Botanical Gardens

- ♥ Bon Secour National Wildlife Refuge

- ♥ Bragg-Mitchell Mansion

- ♥ Buck Island Reef National Monument

- ♥ Dauphin Island Park and Beach

♥ Gulf Coast Exploreum Science Center and IMAX Dome Theater

♥ Guntersville Museum and Cultural Center

♥ Horseshoe Trail Christmas Lights Display, Huntsville

♥ Huntsville Botanical Garden

♥ International Motorsports Hall of Fame

♥ J. B. Lovelace Athletic Museum and Hall of Honor

♥ Lake Eufaula

♥ Lake Guntersville

♥ Little River Canyon National Preserve, Fort Payne

♥ Little River State Forest, Atmore

♥ Muscle Shoals Sound Historic Museum

♥ Museum of Mobile

♥ Old Alabama Town

♥ Orange Beach

♥ Paul W. Bryant Museum

♥ Richards-DAR House Museum

♥ Rickwood Caverns

♥ Rickwood Field

♥ Scott And Zelda Fitzgerald Museum

♥ U.S. Space & Rocket Center

♥ USS Alabama Battleship

Romantic Things To Do In Alaska

Couples will enjoy these Alaska attractions offering romantic things to do together and adult romance ideas in this beautiful state.

- ♥ Aik Nu Tours - Wildlife & Whale Watching Cruises
- ♥ Alaska Aviation Heritage Museum
- ♥ Alaska Law Enforcement Museum
- ♥ Alaska Maritime National Wildlife Refuge
- ♥ Alaska Native Heritage Center
- ♥ Alaska Riverboat Discovery
- ♥ Alaska State Fair
- ♥ Alaska State Museum
- ♥ Alaska Zoo
- ♥ Alyeska Ski Resort
- ♥ Anchorage Community Theatre
- ♥ Anchorage Museum of History & Art
- ♥ Chugach State Park
- ♥ Denali National Park
- ♥ Earthquake Park
- ♥ Fairbanks Summer Arts Festival
- ♥ Goose Lake Park
- ♥ Holy Family Cathedral
- ♥ Horse Drawn Carriage Co, Inc.
- ♥ Jewel Lake
- ♥ Kenai Fjords Tours - glacier tour or wild life cruise.
- ♥ Kincaid Outdoor Center
- ♥ Lake Hood Harbor
- ♥ Lynn Ary Park

♥ Norman Lowell Studio & Gallery, Homer

♥ Point Bridget State Park

♥ Point Woronzof

♥ Potter's Marsh Bird Sanctuary

♥ Temsco Helicopters

♥ Tony Knowles Coastal Trail

♥ University of Alaska Museum

♥ Westchester Lagoon Overlook

Romantic Things To Do in Arizona

Fun things to do in Arizona for couples. Arizona vacations offer outdoor adventure, cheap romantic ideas and time to spend with your soulmate exploring the state.

♥ Arboretum at Flagstaff

♥ Arizona Science Center

♥ Arizona-Sonora Desert Museum

♥ Bell Rock

♥ Camelback Mountain

♥ Canyon Lake

♥ Catalina State Park

♥ Chapel of the Holy Cross

♥ Chase Field

♥ Coconino National Forest

♥ Desert Botanical Gardens

♥ Flagstaff's Historic Downtown

♥ Goldfield Ghost Town

- ♥ Grand Canyon
- ♥ Kitt Peak National Observatory
- ♥ McCormick-Stillman Railroad Park
- ♥ Montezuma's Castle
- ♥ Oak Creek Canyon
- ♥ O.K. Corral
- ♥ Out of Africa Wildlife Park
- ♥ Phoenix Art Museum
- ♥ Pima Air & Space Museum
- ♥ Red Rock Biplane Tours
- ♥ Red Rock State Park
- ♥ Reid Park Zoo
- ♥ Sabino Canyon
- ♥ St. Mary's Basilica - exchange romantic wedding vows.
- ♥ Santa Catalina Mountains
- ♥ Scottsdale Museum Of Contemporary Art
- ♥ Sedona Heritage Museum
- ♥ Skydive Arizona
- ♥ South Mountain Park Scenic Drive
- ♥ Stuffington Bear Factory
- ♥ Temple of Music and Art
- ♥ Trail Dust Town
- ♥ Tucson Botanical Gardens
- ♥ Walnut Canyon National Monument

♥ Water World Safari

♥ Wupatki National Monument

Romantic Things To Do In Arkansas

These Arkansas attractions offer couples fun and creative dating ideas.

Enjoy romantic Arkansas with your soulmate.

♥ Arkansas Arts Center

♥ Arkansas Travelers Baseball Team

♥ Arkansas Walk of Fame

♥ Belle of Hot Springs Riverboat

♥ Buckstaff Bath House

♥ Clayton House

♥ Ducks in the Park - land & water tour.

♥ Eureka Springs Gardens

♥ Garvan Woodland Gardens

♥ Great Passion Play

♥ Historic Arkansas Museum

♥ Hot Springs Mountain Tower

♥ Hot Springs National Park

♥ Hurricane River Cave

♥ Julius Breckling Riverfront Park

♥ Lake Catherine State Park

♥ Lake Dardanelle State Park

♥ Little Rock Tours

♥ Maumelle Park

- ♥ Maxwell Blade Theater of Magic

- ♥ Old State House Museum

- ♥ Petit Jean

- ♥ Pine Mountain Jamboree

- ♥ Pinnacle Mountain State Park

- ♥ Pivot Rock and Natural Bridge

- ♥ Pugh's Mill Park

- ♥ Queen Anne Mansion and Wings

- ♥ Riverfest

- ♥ St. Elizabeth's Catholic Church

- ♥ Turpentine Creek Exotic Wildlife Refuge

- ♥ War Eagle Mill

- ♥ William J. Clinton Presidential Center

Romantic Things To Do in California

Fun things to do in California for couples. If you're looking for cute Valentines day ideas or engagement ideas, you'll find great ones here.

- ♥ Alcatraz Island

- ♥ Aquarium of the Pacific, Los Angeles

- ♥ Artesa Winery, Napa

- ♥ Balboa Park

- ♥ Baywood Cellars Tasting Room, Monterey

- ♥ Bridalveil Falls Day Hike in Yosemite

- ♥ California Palace of the Legion of Honor, San Francisco

- ♥ California Science Center, Los Angeles

- ♥ California State Railroad Museum
- ♥ Coronado Island
- ♥ Crocker Art Museum, Sacramento
- ♥ Disneyland
- ♥ Exploratorium, San Francisco
- ♥ Fabulous Palm Springs Follies
- ♥ Fisherman's Wharf
- ♥ Gaslamp Quarter, San Diego
- ♥ Getty Center
- ♥ Golden Gate Bridge
- ♥ Golden Gate Park
- ♥ Grace Cathedral, San Francisco
- ♥ Grauman's Chinese Theatre
- ♥ Griffith Observatory, Los Angeles
- ♥ Hollywood Sign
- ♥ Holy Virgin Cathedral, San Francisco
- ♥ Indian Canyons, Palm Springs
- ♥ Japanese Friendship Garden, San Jose
- ♥ Japanese Tea Garden
- ♥ La Brea Tar Pits, Los Angeles
- ♥ La Jolla Caves
- ♥ Leo Carrillo State Beach, Los Angeles
- ♥ Little Italy District, San Diego
- ♥ Lombard Street, San Francisco

- ♥ Los Angeles County Museum of Art

- ♥ Mariposa Grove, Yosemite

- ♥ Maritime Museum of San Diego

- ♥ McKinley Park, Sacramento

- ♥ Mission Beach, San Diego

- ♥ Monterey Bay Aquarium

- ♥ Monterey State Historic Park

- ♥ Moonlight Beach, Encinitas

- ♥ Moorten Botanical Garden, Palm Springs

- ♥ Mount Soledad, San Diego

- ♥ Muir Woods National Monument

- ♥ Old Sacramento

- ♥ Palace of Fine Arts, San Francisco

- ♥ Palm Springs Aerial Tramway

- ♥ Rosicrucian Egyptian Museum & Planetarium, San Jose

- ♥ Sacramento Zoo

- ♥ San Diego Zoo

- ♥ Santa Cruz Beach Boardwalk

- ♥ Santa Monica Drive-in At The Pier

- ♥ SeaWorld Adventure Park

- ♥ Six Flags Magic Mountain

- ♥ The Walk of Fame

- ♥ Tunnel View in Yosemite Valley

- ♥ V. Sattui Winery, St Helena

♥ Wild Animal Park, Escondido

♥ Zuma Beach, Malibu

Romantic Things To Do In Colorado

Things to do in Colorado for couples.

Romantic Colorado offers great outdoor fun perfect for free dates, romantic fun and time together.

♥ Alpine Slide, Steamboat Springs

♥ Anheuser-Busch Brewery Tours

♥ Bar D Chuckwagon, Durango

♥ Bear Creek Lake Park, Lakewood

♥ Boulder Falls

♥ Buffalo Bill Memorial Museum & Grave

♥ Carousel Dinner Theatre, Fort Collins

♥ Cave of the Winds, Manitou Springs

♥ Chautauqua Park, Boulder

♥ Cheyenne Mountain Zoo

♥ Colorado National Monument

♥ Coors Brewing Company

♥ Denver Botanic Gardens

♥ Denver Museum of Nature and Science

♥ Denver Zoo

♥ Estes Park Aerial Tramway

♥ Flagstaff Mountain

♥ Four Mile Historic Park, Denver

- ♥ Garden of The Gods

- ♥ Glen Eyrie

- ♥ Glenwood Caverns and Historic Fairy Caves

- ♥ Independence Pass, Aspen

- ♥ Iron Springs Chateau Melodrama and Dinner Theatre, Manitou Springs

- ♥ Lakeside Amusement Park, Denver

- ♥ Larimer Square, Denver

- ♥ Maroon Bells, Aspen

- ♥ Mother Cabrini Shrine, Golden

- ♥ New Belgium Brewing Company

- ♥ North Cheyenne Canyon Park

- ♥ Pikes Peak

- ♥ Pikes Peak Mountain Bike Tours

- ♥ Pro Rodeo Hall of Fame

- ♥ Red Runner Dog Sled Tours, Steamboat Springs

- ♥ Saint Elizabeth Of Hungary, Denver

- ♥ Silver Queen Gondola

- ♥ US Olympic Complex, Colorado Springs

- ♥ Will Rogers Shrine of the Sun

Romantic Things To Do In Connecticut

These Connecticut attractions offer free romantic date ideas, fun night date ideas and awesome views of lighthouses, sea animals and sunsets.

Enjoy these Connecticut activities with your soulmate.

- ♥ B.F. Clyde's Cider Mill

- ♥ Captain John's Nature Cruises, Waterford

- ♥ Connecticut College Arboretum

- ♥ Downeast Lighthouse Cruises, Groton

- ♥ Downtown Cabaret Theatre, Bridgeport

- ♥ Eli Whitney Museum

- ♥ Fort Griswold Battlefield State Park

- ♥ Harriet Beecher Stowe House

- ♥ Lake Compounce Theme Park

- ♥ Leffingwell House Historic Museum

- ♥ Lourdes in Litchfield Shrine of Our Lady of Lourdes

- ♥ Maritime Aquarium at Norwalk

- ♥ Mark Twain House

- ♥ Mystic Aquarium

- ♥ New London Waterfront Park

- ♥ Northwest Park, Windsor

- ♥ Peabody Museum of Natural History

- ♥ Rocky Neck State Park

- ♥ Saint Joseph's Roman Catholic Church, Bristol

- ♥ Shaw Perkins Mansion

- ♥ Shoreline Trolley Museum

- ♥ Spirit of Broadway Theater

- ♥ U.S. Coast Guard Academy

- ♥ Voyager Cruises, Mystic

- ♥ Wickham Park

♥ Yale University Art Gallery

Romantic Things To Do In Delaware

These romantic things to do in Delaware for couples offer sunsets over Delaware beaches, fun date ideas and love in the summer sun.

♥ Abbott's Mill Nature Center

♥ Ballet Theater of Dover

♥ Bellevue State Park

♥ Bethany Beach

♥ Biggs Museum of American Art

♥ Bombay Hook National Wildlife Refuge

♥ Cape Henlopen State Park

♥ Cape May-Lewes Ferry

♥ Chapel Street Playhouse, Newark

♥ Christina River Boat Company, Wilmington

♥ Coastal Kayak & Sailing, Betheny Beach

♥ Corks Point Outdoors, Smyrna

♥ Delaware Agriculture Museum and Village, Dover

♥ Delaware Ghost Tours, New Castle

♥ Delaware Museum of Natural History

♥ Delaware Seashore State Park

♥ Delaware Shakespeare Festival

♥ Delaware Sports Museum and Hall of Fame

♥ Dewey Beach

♥ Dover Symphony Orchestra

- ♥ DuPont Nature Center

- ♥ DuPont Theatre

- ♥ Elsie Williams Doll Collection, Georgetown

- ♥ Fenwick Beach

- ♥ First State Ballet Theatre, Wilmington

- ♥ Gibraltar (Marian Coffin Gardens)

- ♥ Great Delaware Kite Festival

- ♥ Hagley Museum and Library

- ♥ Lewes Beach

- ♥ Nassau Valley Vineyards & Winery

- ♥ Nemours Mansion & Gardens, Wilmington

- ♥ Prime Hook National Wildlife Refuge, Milton

- ♥ Rehoboth Beach

- ♥ Riverfront Wilmington

- ♥ Scenic Biplane Rides, Dover

- ♥ Wilmington and Western Railroad

Romantic Things To Do In Florida

These things to do in Florida offer couples fun first dates, one day road trips or weekend romantic getaways in Florida.

- ♥ Ancient Spanish Monastery

- ♥ Anne Kolb Nature Center

- ♥ Bahia Honda State Park

- ♥ Billie Swamp Safari, Clewiston

- ♥ Bill's Airboat Adventures, Oviedo

- ♥ Boggy Creek Airboat & Swamp Buggy Rides
- ♥ Bok Tower Gardens
- ♥ Busch Gardens
- ♥ Captain Anderson's Marina, Panama City
- ♥ Caribbean Gardens
- ♥ Castillo de San Marcos
- ♥ Coral Castle
- ♥ Corkscrew Swamp Sanctuary
- ♥ Cummer Museum of Art & Gardens
- ♥ Daytona
- ♥ Deering Estate, Miami
- ♥ Dry Tortugas National Park
- ♥ Everglades National Park
- ♥ Fort Caroline National Memorial
- ♥ Gatorland
- ♥ Hollywood Beach Boardwalk
- ♥ Honeymoon Island State Park
- ♥ Jacksonville Zoo and Gardens
- ♥ Jungle Queen Riverboat, Fort Lauderdale
- ♥ Lightner Museum, St Augustine
- ♥ Mel Fisher Maritime Heritage Museum
- ♥ Miami Dade Eco-Adventure Tours
- ♥ Morikami Museum & Japanese Gardens
- ♥ Nancy Forrester's Secret Garden

- ♥ Old Florida Museum, St. Augustine

- ♥ Old Town, Kissimmee

- ♥ Riverfront Cruises, Fort Lauderdale

- ♥ Riverwalk, Jacksonville

- ♥ Salvador Dali Museum

- ♥ San Sebastian Winery

- ♥ SeaWorld Orlando

- ♥ SkyScapes Balloon Tours, Belle Isle

- ♥ South Beach

- ♥ Southern Star Dolphin & Sunset Cruises, Destin

- ♥ St. Andrew's State Park

- ♥ St. Augustine Lighthouse & Museum

- ♥ Sunken Gardens, St. Petersburg

- ♥ The Zoo, Gulf Breeze

- ♥ Universal Studios Florida

- ♥ Walt Disney World

- ♥ Yuengling Brewery

Romantic Things To Do In Georgia

Georgia vacations offer great date ideas for couples indoors and outdoors.

Georgia attractions are many with opportunities for romance throughout the state.

- ♥ Atlanta Botanical Gardens

- ♥ Atlanta Braves

- ♥ Atlanta History Center

- ♥ Blythe Island Regional Park

- ♥ Charlemagne's Kingdom, Helen

- ♥ Chehaw Wild Animal Park

- ♥ Donna Van Gogh's Artists Market, Atlanta

- ♥ Fernbank Museum of Natural History

- ♥ Fort Pulaski National Monument

- ♥ Georgia Aquarium

- ♥ Grand Opera House, Macon

- ♥ Juliette Gordon Low Birthplace

- ♥ Lake Winnepesaukah Amusement Park

- ♥ Margaret Mitchell House & Museum

- ♥ Martin Luther King, Jr. National Historic Site

- ♥ Nora Mill Granary Grist Mill & Country Store, Helen

- ♥ Oktoberfest, Savannah

- ♥ Old Fort Jackson Historic Site

- ♥ Old Town Trolley Tours, Savannah

- ♥ Owens-Thomas House, Savannah

- ♥ Piedmont Park

- ♥ Pine Mountain Wild Animal Safari

- ♥ Providence Canyon State Park, Columbus

- ♥ Savannah History Museum

- ♥ Sea Kayak Georgia, Tybee Island

- ♥ Ships of the Sea Maritime Museum

- ♥ St. Simons Island Lighthouse

- ♥ Sweet Water Brewery Company

- ♥ Tybee Island Lighthouse

- ♥ UGA Cohutta Fisheries Center

- ♥ University of Georgia Marine Education Center and Aquarium

- ♥ World of Coca-Cola

- ♥ Wormsloe State Historic Site

Romantic Things To Do In Hawaii

Big Island

- ♥ 'Ahanalui Pool

- ♥ Air tours

- ♥ Anaeho'omalu Beach

- ♥ ATV Outfitters - tours

- ♥ Bike volcano tours

- ♥ Blue Sea Cruises - scenic cruises

- ♥ Capt. Cook Monument

- ♥ Coconut Island Park

- ♥ Coffee tasting tours

- ♥ Dive or snorkel with manta rays

- ♥ Dolphin tours

- ♥ Gardens at Nani Mau

- ♥ Glass bottomed boat tours

- ♥ Hamakua Coast

- ♥ Hapuna Beach

- ♥ Helicopter tours

- ♥ Hilo's Coral Reef Discovery Center
- ♥ Hilo's Pana'ewa Rainforest Zoo & Gardens
- ♥ Horseback tours
- ♥ Isaac Hale Beach Park
- ♥ Jet ski
- ♥ Kauna'oa Beach
- ♥ Kapoho Tide Pools
- ♥ Ka'upulehu Beach
- ♥ Kayak tours
- ♥ Laupahoehoe Train Museum and Visitors Center
- ♥ Lava tours
- ♥ Mackenzie State Park
- ♥ Ocean Rider, Inc - seahorse tour
- ♥ Parker Ranch
- ♥ Pua Mau Place
- ♥ Puna Coast
- ♥ Punalu'u Beach Park - black sand beach
- ♥ Reef tours
- ♥ Scuba or snuba
- ♥ Submarine tours
- ♥ Volcanoes National Park
- ♥ Volcano tours
- ♥ Volcano Winery
- ♥ Waterfall helihike

- ♥ Whale watch

- ♥ Windsurf

- ♥ Zipline

Kauai

- ♥ Ahukini Pier

- ♥ ATV tours

- ♥ Bridges of Hanalei

- ♥ Coconut Coast

- ♥ Fern Grotto

- ♥ Flightseeing tours

- ♥ Go bodyboarding

- ♥ Go rafting

- ♥ Grove Farm Homestead

- ♥ Hanalei Bay

- ♥ Helicopter tours

- ♥ Hideaway's Beach

- ♥ Hike to Hanakapiai Falls

- ♥ Kauai Coffee Visitor Center

- ♥ Kauai Museum in Lihu'e

- ♥ Kayak the Wailua River

- ♥ Ke'ahua Arboretum

- ♥ Ke'e Beach

- ♥ Kitesurf

- ♥ Lydgate Beach Park

- ♥ Maniniholo Dry Cave

- ♥ Na 'Aina Kai Botanical Gardens

- ♥ Mountain bike tours

- ♥ Outfitters Kauai - snorkel, surf, swim, zipline

- ♥ Po'ipu Beach Park

- ♥ Scuba diving

- ♥ Silver Falls Ranch horseback tours

- ♥ Skydive

- ♥ Snorkel cruises

- ♥ Spouting Horn

- ♥ Sunset dinner sails

- ♥ Tour on a motorcycle

- ♥ Waimea Canyon

Maui

- ♥ Alexander & Baldwin Sugar Museum

- ♥ Bailey House Museum

- ♥ Big Beach - off old Makena Highway.

- ♥ Bike tours

- ♥ Blue Water Rafting - explore sea caves.

- ♥ Dig Me Beach - Ka'anapali

- ♥ D.T. Fleming Beach

- ♥ Go paragliding

- ♥ Go scuba diving

- ♥ Haleakala National Park

- ♥ Hana Lava Tube
- ♥ Hawaiian Sailing Canoe Adventures
- ♥ Hike
- ♥ Ho'okipa Beach
- ♥ Kahanu Garden
- ♥ Kapalua Beach
- ♥ Kayak
- ♥ Kealia Pond National Wildlife Refuge
- ♥ Kitesurf
- ♥ Kula Botanical Gardens
- ♥ Lahaina Legends & Lore History Cruise
- ♥ Lana'i Wild Dolphin & Snorkel Eco-Adventure
- ♥ Maui Canyon Adventures - offers rapelling
- ♥ Maui Dive Shop for a sunset dinner cruise.
- ♥ Maui Pineapple Company
- ♥ Moloka'i
- ♥ Ocean Science Center
- ♥ Ohe'o Gulch
- ♥ Pacific Whale Foundation tidepool exploration program
- ♥ Parasail
- ♥ Red Sand Beach
- ♥ Snorkel tour
- ♥ Stargazing cruises
- ♥ Sugar Cane Train

♥ Take a helicopter tour

♥ Take a horseback tour

♥ Tedeschi Winery

♥ Waikamoi Preserve

♥ Wai'anapanapa State Park

♥ Whale watch tour

♥ Zipline in a rainforest

Oahu

♥ Aloha Tower piers - dinner cruises

♥ Atlantis Adventures - submarine tour

♥ Chinatown

♥ Dole Plantation

♥ Diamond Head

♥ Dolphin Excursions

♥ Foster Botanical Garden

♥ Go parasailing

♥ Go surfing

♥ Haiku Gardens

♥ Hale'iwa Surf Museum

♥ Hanauma Bay Nature Park

♥ Hawaii Kai Marina

♥ Hawaiian Waters Adventure Park

♥ Honolulu Academy of Arts

♥ Honolulu Zoo

- ♥ Ho'omaluhia Botanical Gardens
- ♥ 'Iolani Palace
- ♥ Kailua Bay
- ♥ Kane'ohe Bay
- ♥ Lyon Arboretum
- ♥ Makapu'u Lighthouse Trail - you can whale watch, too.
- ♥ Moanalua Gardens
- ♥ National Cemetery of the Pacific
- ♥ Oahu Ghost Tours
- ♥ Pacific Aviation Museum
- ♥ Pearl Harbor
- ♥ Plantation Village
- ♥ Polynesian Cultural Center
- ♥ Scuba dive
- ♥ Snorkel
- ♥ Take a biplane ride
- ♥ Take a glider ride
- ♥ Take a guided horseback tour
- ♥ Take a guided mountain bike tour
- ♥ Take a helicopter tour
- ♥ Take a walking tour
- ♥ The Contemporary Museum
- ♥ U.S. Army Museum
- ♥ USS Bowfin Submarine Museum and Park

- ♥ Valley of the Temples Memorial Park

- ♥ Waikiki Aquarium

- ♥ Waikiki Beach

- ♥ Waimanalo Bay Recreational Center and Beach Park

- ♥ Waterfall hikes and tours

Things To Do In Idaho For Couples

- ♥ Aggipah River Trips

- ♥ Basque Museum & Cultural Center

- ♥ Boise Mormon Temple

- ♥ Boise River Greenbelt

- ♥ Boise River Rafting

- ♥ Boise Train Depot

- ♥ Boise Trolley Tours

- ♥ Camel's Back Park

- ♥ Canyon County Historical Society & Museum

- ♥ Cathedral of St. John the Evangelist

- ♥ Ceramica, Boise

- ♥ Discovery Center of Idaho

- ♥ Hyde Park

- ♥ Idaho Botanical Garden

- ♥ Idaho State Historical Museum

- ♥ Indian Creek Winery

- ♥ Lake Pend Oreille

- ♥ Meridian Speedway

♥ Montana Rockies Rail Tours, Sandpoint

♥ Morrison-Knudsen Nature Center

♥ Old Idaho Penitentiary

♥ Pend d'Oreille Winery, Sandpoint

♥ Ridge to Rivers Trail System, Boise

♥ Roaring Springs Water Park

♥ Sandpoint City Beach

♥ Snake River Birds of Prey National Conservation Area

♥ Sun Valley Jazz Jamboree

♥ Trophy Trout Charters

♥ Warhawk Air Museum

♥ Warm Springs Avenue, Boise

♥ World Center for Birds of Prey

♥ Zoo Boise

Things To Do In Illinois For Couples

These Illinois attractions offer lots of Illinois things to do for couples. Send your sweetie some love text messages then set off on seeking romance in this romantic state.

♥ Anderson Japanese Gardens

♥ Art Institute of Chicago

♥ Beer Nuts and Bloomington Sale Barn

♥ Brookfield Zoo

♥ Chicago Botanic Garden

♥ Chicago Trolley Tours

♥ Clarence Buckingham Fountain

- ♥ Crab Orchard Lake

- ♥ Dana-Thomas House State Historic Site

- ♥ Field Museum, Chicago

- ♥ Frank Lloyd Wright Home & Studio

- ♥ Galena Trolley Depot Theatre

- ♥ Grant Park

- ♥ Greektown

- ♥ Handmade On Main, Algonquin

- ♥ Historic Barn Tours, Macomb

- ♥ Krape Park, Freeport

- ♥ Lincoln Home National Historic Site

- ♥ Lincoln Park Conservatory

- ♥ Lincoln Park Zoo

- ♥ LinMar Gardens

- ♥ Magic Waters Waterpark

- ♥ Medieval Times Dinner & Tournament, Schaumburg

- ♥ Millennium Park

- ♥ Miller Park Zoo

- ♥ Morton Arboretum

- ♥ Museum of Science and Industry

- ♥ National Shrine of Our Lady of the Snows

- ♥ O'Leary's Fire Truck Tours, Chicago

- ♥ Our Lady of Sorrows Basilica

- ♥ River Cruises on the Twilight, Galena

♥ Six Flags Great America

♥ Spirit of Peoria

♥ Tower Park, Peoria

♥ Ulysses S. Grant Home

♥ University of Chicago

♥ Walter Payton's Roundhouse Complex

♥ Wendella Sightseeing Boats, Chicago

♥ William M. Staerkel Planetarium

♥ Willis Tower (formerly Sears Tower) Skydeck

♥ Wrigley Field Tours

Things To Do In Indiana For Couples

Things to do in Indiana with your soulmate. If you're looking for marriage proposals ideas or to rekindle romance, you'll find good ideas here.

♥ American Cabaret Theatre

♥ Cardinal Greenway

♥ Chateau Thomas Winery

♥ Clifty Falls

♥ East Race Waterway

♥ Foellinger-Freimann Botanical Conservatory

♥ George Rogers Clark National Historical Park

♥ Hoosier Park

♥ Indianapolis Indians Baseball

♥ International Friendship Gardens

♥ Lanier Mansion State Historic Site

- ♥ Mainstreet Theatre

- ♥ Mesker Park Zoo & Botanic Garden

- ♥ Monroe Lake

- ♥ Morris Performing Arts Center

- ♥ Northern Indiana Center for History

- ♥ Oliver Winery

- ♥ Pines Peak Family Ski Area

- ♥ Rapid Raceway, Angola

- ♥ Science Central

- ♥ Scottish Rite Cathedral

- ♥ Shadyside Memorial Park

- ♥ Strawberry Festival

- ♥ Sunset Hill Farm County Park

- ♥ Thomas Family Winery

- ♥ Track Attack Racing School

- ♥ Tropicanoe Cove

- ♥ Washington Park Zoo

- ♥ Wesselman Woods Nature Preserve

Romantic Things To Do In Iowa

Ideas for things to do in Iowa. If you're looking for ideas for a fun date, romantic proposal ideas, or just some relationship rescue from the stresses of every day life, you'll find fun and romance in Iowa.

- ♥ Airline Amusement Park

- ♥ Basilica of St. John

- ♥ Bellevue Butterfly Garden

- ♥ Blank Park Zoo
- ♥ Burlington Bees Professional Baseball
- ♥ Cedar Falls Community Theatre
- ♥ Crystal Lake Cave
- ♥ Des Moines Botanical Center
- ♥ Dorothy Pecaut Nature Center
- ♥ Dubuque Arboretum and Botanical Gardens
- ♥ Fenelon Place Elevator
- ♥ Field of Dreams, Dubuque
- ♥ Historic General Dodge House
- ♥ Indian Creek Nature Center
- ♥ Iowa Rock 'n' Roll Music Association Museum
- ♥ Iowa State Capitol
- ♥ Iowa State University
- ♥ Iowa Valley Scenic Byway
- ♥ Lee County Speedway
- ♥ Lewis and Clark Monument
- ♥ Lost Island Waterpark
- ♥ Mathias Ham House
- ♥ Nathaniel Hamlin Park and Museum
- ♥ National Motorcycle Museum
- ♥ Old Fort Madison
- ♥ Prairie Moon Winery and Vineyards
- ♥ Quad City Arts Festival of Trees

- ♥ Reiman Gardens

- ♥ Seminole Valley Farm

- ♥ Sergeant Floyd Monument

- ♥ Seven Oaks

- ♥ Squirrel Cage Jail

- ♥ Stone State Park

- ♥ Tabor Home Vineyards & Winery

- ♥ Theatre Cedar Rapids

- ♥ Trinity Heights

- ♥ Ushers Ferry Historic Village

Things To Do In Kansas For Couples

Romantic things to do in Kansas. Kansas vacations offer couples romance ideas in the great outdoors, on walking tours or in museums and theaters.

- ♥ Abilene and Smokey Valley Railroad

- ♥ Botanica, The Wichita Gardens

- ♥ Campanile Bell Tower

- ♥ Campbell Castle

- ♥ Carlson's Corn Maze and Wildflower Tours

- ♥ Central Mall Aquarium, Salina

- ♥ Coronado Heights and Spanish Castle

- ♥ Crown Uptown Professional Dinner Theatre

- ♥ Dorothy's House, Liberal

- ♥ Downtown Lawrence

- ♥ Equifest of Kansas

- ♥ Exploration Place
- ♥ Fort Scott Jubilee
- ♥ Gage Park Mini-Train
- ♥ Great Plains Nature Center
- ♥ Great Plains Theatre Festival, Abilene
- ♥ Greyhound Hall of Fame
- ♥ Holton Walking Tour
- ♥ Hutchinson Zoo
- ♥ Kansas Expocentre
- ♥ Kansas State University
- ♥ Kansas Vietnam Veterans Memorial
- ♥ Konza Prairie Research Natural Area
- ♥ Lakeside Speedway
- ♥ Lawrence Community Theatre
- ♥ Lebold Mansion
- ♥ Memorial Hall, Kansas City
- ♥ Milford Lake
- ♥ Overland Park Arboretum and Botanical Garden
- ♥ Ralph Mitchell Zoo and Riverside Park
- ♥ Reinisch Rose Garden
- ♥ Rolling Hills Refuge Wildlife Center
- ♥ Russell Stover Candy Outlet
- ♥ Sedgwick County Zoo
- ♥ Smoky Hill Vineyards and Winery

- ♥ Theatre Atchison

- ♥ Topeka Zoological Park

- ♥ Tuttle Creek Lake

- ♥ Vaniman Mansion

- ♥ Wyandotte County Lake and Park

- ♥ Yoder Amish Community, Hutchinson

Things To Do In Kentucky For Couples

Things to do in Kentucky for couples. Perfect for romantic birthday ideas and romantic date ideas.

- ♥ A Salute to Country Music Legends, Cave City

- ♥ Abbey of Gethsemani, Bardstown

- ♥ Abraham Lincoln Birthplace National Historic Site

- ♥ Alben W. Barkley Museum, Paducah

- ♥ Beech Bend Raceway Park

- ♥ Belle of Louisville/Spirit of Jefferson

- ♥ Benjamin Henry Latrobe's Pope Villa

- ♥ Bob Noble Park

- ♥ Brennan House & Medical Office Museum

- ♥ Brown-Pusey House

- ♥ Buffalo Trace Distillery

- ♥ Capitol Arts Center, Bowling Green

- ♥ Cathedral of the Assumption, Louisville

- ♥ Classic Biplane Tours, Louisville

- ♥ Constitution Square State Historic Site

- ♥ Crystal Onyx Cave

- ♥ Daniel Boone National Forest

- ♥ Demonstration & Trial Garden, Paducah

- ♥ E.P. Tom Sawyer State Park

- ♥ Farmington Historic House

- ♥ Felice Vineyards

- ♥ Herb Farm at Strodes Run

- ♥ Historic Homes & Landmarks Tour of Lebanon

- ♥ Horse Farm Tours - Lexington

- ♥ Huber's Orchard & Winery, Louisville

- ♥ Kentucky Confederate Studies Archives

- ♥ Kentucky Derby

- ♥ Kentucky State Fair

- ♥ Kentucky Shakespeare Festival

- ♥ Liberty Hall

- ♥ Lincoln Statue, Elizabethtown

- ♥ Louisville Zoo

- ♥ Mary Todd Lincoln House

- ♥ McConnell Springs, Lexington

- ♥ My Old Kentucky Home State Park, Bardstown

- ♥ Newport Aquarium

- ♥ Old Bardstown Village

- ♥ Paducah International Raceway

- ♥ Paducah Wall to Wall Murals

- ♥ Riverview at Hobson Grove

- ♥ Saint Joseph's Proto-Cathedral, Bardstown

- ♥ Simpson County Archives & Museum

- ♥ Six Flags Kentucky Kingdom

- ♥ Springhill Winery, Bardstown

- ♥ St. Martin of Tours Catholic Church, Louisville

- ♥ Star of Louisville - scenic cruises

- ♥ The Arboretum - State Botanical Garden

- ♥ Thomas Edison House

- ♥ Waterfront Park, Louisville

- ♥ Woodford Reserve Distillery

Things To Do In Louisiana For Couples

Things to do in Louisiana for couples. These places are perfect for romantic anniversary ideas, romantic dates and romantic vacations.

- ♥ Alexandria Zoological Park

- ♥ American Aquatic Gardens

- ♥ Angola Prison Rodeo, St Francisville

- ♥ Aquarium Of The Americas

- ♥ Audubon Zoo

- ♥ Barnwell Memorial Garden and Art Center

- ♥ Baton Rouge Zoo

- ♥ Bayou Black Airboat Swamp Tours, Houma

- ♥ Bayou Pierre Alligator Park

- ♥ Beauregard-Keyes House, New Orleans

- ♥ Biedenharn Museum and Gardens
- ♥ Butler Greenwood Plantation, St Francisville
- ♥ Cabildo
- ♥ Cajun Pride Swamp Tour, Laplace
- ♥ Cathedral of St John the Evangelist, Lafayette
- ♥ Cole Pratt Gallery, New Orleans
- ♥ Elms Mansion
- ♥ Gardens of the American Rose Center
- ♥ Greenwood Plantation, St Francisville
- ♥ Haunted History Tours, New Orleans
- ♥ Kiroli Park, West Monroe
- ♥ Kliebert's Turtle and Alligator Tours, Hammond
- ♥ Lake Fausse Pointe State Park
- ♥ Lincoln Parish Park
- ♥ Longue Vue House & Gardens
- ♥ Louisiana's Old State Capitol
- ♥ Mardi Gras World
- ♥ Melrose Plantation, Natchitoches
- ♥ Memorial Hall - Confederate Civil War Museum
- ♥ Musee Conti Wax Museum
- ♥ Museum of the American Cocktail
- ♥ Myrtles Plantation, St Francisville
- ♥ Natchez Steamboat
- ♥ National D-Day Museum

♥ New Orleans Museum Of Art

♥ Oakley House - Audubon State Historic Site

♥ Rip Van Winkle Gardens

♥ Sam Houston Jones State Park

♥ Shreveport Metropolitan Ballet

♥ Skydive Louisiana, Shreveport

♥ Spirit of the Red River Cruise, Shreveport

♥ St. Louis Cathedral, New Orleans

♥ St. Valerie Shrine, Thibodaux

♥ USS KIDD Veterans Memorial Museum

Things To Do In Maine For Couples

Things to do in Maine for couples including romantic dinner ideas on a sunset cruise. Romantic gestures, romantic words and romantic time with your soulmate await you in Maine.

♥ Acadian Whale Adventures, Bar Harbor

♥ Atlantic Brewing Company

♥ Atlantic Seal Cruises

♥ Balmy Days Cruises, Boothbay Harbor

♥ Bay View Cruises, Portland

♥ Bingo Deep Sea Fishing

♥ Camden Snow Bowl

♥ Carousel Music Theatre, Boothbay Harbor

♥ Department of Marine Resources & Aquarium

♥ Desert of Maine

♥ Kennebunkport Marina

- ♥ Lily Hill Farm

- ♥ Lucky Catch Cruises

- ♥ Lulu Lobster Boat Ride, Bar Harbor

- ♥ Maine Discovery Museum

- ♥ Moose Point State Park

- ♥ National Park Sea Kayak Tours

- ♥ Our Lady of Good Hope Catholic Church

- ♥ Pine Haven Winter Park

- ♥ Portland Observatory

- ♥ Schooner Olad

- ♥ Sea Venture Custom Boat Tours

- ♥ Shipyard Brewing Company

- ♥ State of Maine Cheese Company

- ♥ Tate House Museum

- ♥ Thorncrag Bird Sanctuary

- ♥ Tidal Transit Ocean Kayak & Bike Company

- ♥ Victoria Mansion, Portland

Things To Do In Maryland For Couples

These things to do in Maryland for couples offer romantic evening ideas and romantic ideas for anniversary or birthdays.

- ♥ American Visionary Art Museum

- ♥ Annapolis Art Walk

- ♥ Antietam National Battlefield

- ♥ Assateague Island Explorer

- ♥ B & O Railroad Museum

- ♥ Baltimore Civil War Museum

- ♥ Baltimore Maritime Museum

- ♥ Baltimore Museum of Art

- ♥ Belair Mansion

- ♥ C&O Canal National Park Exhibit Center

- ♥ Candlelight Ghost Tours of Frederick

- ♥ Chesapeake & Ohio Canal National Historical Park

- ♥ Chesapeake Bay Skipjack Rebecca T. Ruark Charters

- ♥ Choptank River Fishing Pier

- ♥ Easton Point Marina

- ♥ Edgar Allan Poe House and Museum

- ♥ Fort McHenry National Monument and Historic Shrine

- ♥ Frederick Tour & Carriage Company

- ♥ Frontier Town Western Theme Park

- ♥ Gilbert Run Park

- ♥ Great Falls Park

- ♥ Hargerstown City Park

- ♥ Hessian Barracks

- ♥ Historic B&O Train Station

- ♥ Inner Harbor & Harbor Cruise

- ♥ Lacrosse Hall of Fame Museum

- ♥ Maryland Science Center

- ♥ McCrillis Gardens

♥ Milburn Orchards

♥ Montpelier Mansion

♥ National Aquarium in Baltimore

♥ National Museum of Dentistry

♥ Ocean City Pier Rides & Amusements

♥ Ocean City Sky Tours

♥ Oriole Park At Camden Yards

♥ Poplar Hill Mansion

♥ Port Discovery

♥ Salisbury Zoo & Park

♥ Sandy Point State Park

♥ Schifferstadt Architectural Museum

♥ Schooner Woodwind Sailing Cruises

♥ St. Mary's Roman Catholic Church

♥ Swallow Falls State Park

♥ Talent Machine Company

♥ U.S. Army Ordinance Museum

♥ U.S.S. Constellation

♥ William Paca House and Garden

Things To Do In Massachusetts

Fun things to do in Massachusetts for couples offering romantic ideas for dates and romantic ideas for husband or wives. Enjoy this magnificent state together.

♥ Beacon Hill

♥ Boston By Foot

- ♥ Boston Common
- ♥ Boston Duck Tours
- ♥ Brant Point Light Station
- ♥ Carousel at Battleship Cove
- ♥ Charles River Esplanade
- ♥ Chilmark
- ♥ Chinatown
- ♥ Craigville Beach
- ♥ Davis Square
- ♥ Discovery Adventures Sea Kayaking
- ♥ East Chop Light
- ♥ Edgartown
- ♥ Fame, The Salem Privateer
- ♥ Faneuil Hall Marketplace
- ♥ Flying Horses Carousel
- ♥ Forefather's Monument
- ♥ Freedom Trail
- ♥ Harvard University
- ♥ Haunted Footsteps Ghost Tour
- ♥ Heritage Plantation
- ♥ House of the Seven Gables
- ♥ Hyannis Whale Watcher Cruises
- ♥ Isabella Stewart Gardner Museum
- ♥ Long Point Wildlife Refuge Beach

- ♥ Madaket Beach
- ♥ Man at the Wheel Statue
- ♥ Marblehead Little Theatre
- ♥ Mayflower II
- ♥ MIT Museum
- ♥ Museum of Science
- ♥ Nantucket Historical Association
- ♥ Nantucket Island Tours
- ♥ National Shrine of Divine Mercy
- ♥ New England Aquarium Whale Watch
- ♥ Newbury Street
- ♥ North Shore Music Theatre
- ♥ Paul Revere House
- ♥ Peabody Essex Museum
- ♥ Photo Walk
- ♥ Pilgrim Monument
- ♥ Plymouth Rock
- ♥ Provincetown
- ♥ Provincetown Bike Trails
- ♥ Provincetown Trolley
- ♥ Prudential Center Skywalk Observatory
- ♥ Public Garden, Boston
- ♥ Race Point Beach
- ♥ Salem Trolley

- ♥ Salem Willows

- ♥ Scargo Stoneware Pottery & Art Gallery

- ♥ Scargo Tower

- ♥ Schooner Thomas E. Lannon

- ♥ Swan Boats of Boston

- ♥ Ventfort Hall

- ♥ Whaling Museum, Nantucket

Things To Do In Michigan For Couples

Things to do in Michigan for couples. There's romantic ideas for him, romantic ideas for New Years and lots more.

- ♥ Amber Elk Ranch, Ludington

- ♥ Antique Toy & Firehouse Museum

- ♥ Big Sable Point Lighthouse, Ludington State Park

- ♥ Bowers Harbor Vineyard, Traverse City

- ♥ Charles H. Wright Museum of African American History

- ♥ Comerica Park

- ♥ Cranbrook Art Museum

- ♥ Crossroads Village & Huckleberry Railroad

- ♥ Detroit Institute of Arts

- ♥ Detroit Science Center

- ♥ Detroit Zoo

- ♥ Eagle Harbor Lighthouse, Keweenaw Peninsula

- ♥ Echo Valley, Kalamazoo

- ♥ Edsel & Eleanor Ford House

- ♥ Fishmas Charters, Whitehall
- ♥ Ford Rouge Factory Tour
- ♥ Frankfort North Breakwater Light
- ♥ Frederik Meijer Gardens & Sculpture Park
- ♥ Gerald Ford Museum
- ♥ GM World
- ♥ Grand Haven State Park
- ♥ Grand Rapids Ballet Company
- ♥ Greektown
- ♥ Greenfield Village
- ♥ Hart Plaza, Detroit
- ♥ Henry Ford Estate - Fair Lane
- ♥ Henry Ford Museum
- ♥ Historic Fort Wayne
- ♥ John Ball Zoological Garden
- ♥ Kalamazoo Institute of Art
- ♥ Kensington Metropark
- ♥ Mackinac Island
- ♥ Meadow Brook Hall, Rochester
- ♥ Meridian Historical Village
- ♥ Michigan International Speedway
- ♥ Petoskey Beach
- ♥ Silver Beach, St Joseph
- ♥ Silver Lake Sand Dunes

- ♥ Soo Locks Boat Tours, Sault Ste. Marie

- ♥ St Julian Winery

- ♥ Star of Saugatuck Boat Cruises

- ♥ Stepping Stone Falls, Flint

- ♥ Thorne Swift Nature Preserve

- ♥ Thunder Bay National Underwater Marine Sanctuary, Alpena

- ♥ University of Michigan Matthaei Botanical Gardens

- ♥ University of Michigan Football Stadium

- ♥ Veldeer's Tulip Gardens

- ♥ Woldumar Nature Center, Lansing

- ♥ World's Largest Musical Fountain, Grand Haven

Things To Do In Minnesota For Couples

Things to do in Minnesota for couples perfect for romantic ideas for Valentines Day, birthdays or romantic weekend vacations.

Toast to your love with champagne drinks, enjoy romantic meals together then set out to explore the romantic places in Minnesota.

- ♥ Afton Alps Recreation Area

- ♥ American Swedish Institute

- ♥ Andiamo Showboat

- ♥ Assisi Heights, Rochester

- ♥ Basilica of St. Mary

- ♥ Buena Vista Ski Area

- ♥ Carlos Creek Winery

- ♥ Casey's Amusement Park, Alexandria

- ♥ Cathedral of St Paul

- ♥ Epic Sled Dog Adventures, Duluth
- ♥ Falls of St. Anthony
- ♥ Forestville Mystery Cave
- ♥ Foshay Tower Museum
- ♥ Frederick R.Weisman Art Museum
- ♥ Glensheen Estate
- ♥ Hyland Lake Park Reserve
- ♥ James J. Hill House
- ♥ Lake Calhoun
- ♥ Lake Nokomis
- ♥ Mayowood Mansion
- ♥ Memorial Park Trail, Red Wing
- ♥ Mill City Museum
- ♥ Minneapolis Institute of Arts
- ♥ Minneapolis Sculpture Garden
- ♥ Minnesota History Center
- ♥ Minnesota State Capitol
- ♥ Minnesota Zoo
- ♥ Minnehaha Park and Falls
- ♥ Minneopa State Park
- ♥ Munsinger/Clemens Gardens
- ♥ Normandale Japanese Garden, Bloomington
- ♥ North Shore Scenic Railroad
- ♥ Oliver H Kelley Farm, Elk River

- ♥ Padelford Packet Boat Company - riverboat cruises

- ♥ Park at Mall of America

- ♥ Paul Bunyan's Animal Land

- ♥ Pipestone National Monument Rice Park

- ♥ Rose Garden, Minneapolis

- ♥ Quarry Hill Nature Center

- ♥ Science Museum of Minnesota

- ♥ Sculpture Gardens, Brainerd

- ♥ Stillwater Trolley

- ♥ Stone Arch Bridge

- ♥ Underwater Adventures, Bloomington

- ♥ Uptown Art Fair, Minneapolis

- ♥ Valleyfair Amusement Park

- ♥ Vista Fleet Excursions, Duluth

- ♥ Walker Art Center

Things To Do In Mississippi For Couples

Things to do in Mississippi including romantic ideas for wife and husband to share together plus ideas for a fun date.

- ♥ Alligator Farm and Airboat Rides, Pascagoula

- ♥ Beauvoir - Jefferson Davis's home

- ♥ Cedar Hill Farm, Hernando

- ♥ Corinth Civil War Interpretive Center

- ♥ Dunleith

- ♥ Florewood River Plantation State Park

- ♥ Grand Gulf Military Monument Park
- ♥ Hattieburg Zoo at Kamper Park
- ♥ Jackson Mynelle Gardens
- ♥ L.V. Hull's Ethnic Yard Art, Kosciusko
- ♥ Lake Lowndes State Park
- ♥ La Pointe-Krebs House
- ♥ Lynn Meadows Discovery Center
- ♥ Martha Vick House, Vicksburg
- ♥ Melrose, Natchez
- ♥ Merrehope, Meridian
- ♥ Meridian Zoological Park
- ♥ Mississippi Agricultural and Forestry Museum
- ♥ Mississippi River Tours, Vicksburg
- ♥ Natchez Trace Parkway
- ♥ Old Capitol Museum of Mississippi History
- ♥ Old South Winery, Natchez
- ♥ Rosalie Mansion
- ♥ Southern Belle Fishing Tours, Gulfport
- ♥ Springfield Plantation
- ♥ St. Joseph's Catholic Church, Starkville
- ♥ St. Mary's Basilica
- ♥ Stanton Hall
- ♥ Tunica Queen Riverboat
- ♥ Vicksburg National Military Park

- ♥ Waverley Mansion, West Point

- ♥ Windsor Ruins

- ♥ Wolf Lake and Broad Lake

Things To Do In Missouri For Couples

These things to do in Missouri for couples offer romantic ideas for Valentines day and romantic night ideas.

- ♥ 18th & Vine District, Kansas City

- ♥ Anheuser-Busch Brewery

- ♥ Baldknobbers Theater

- ♥ Bowling Hall of Fame

- ♥ Branson

- ♥ Butterfly House & Education Center

- ♥ Cameron Cave, Hannibal

- ♥ Cathedral Basilica of St. Louis

- ♥ Chatillon-DeMenil Mansion

- ♥ City Museum, St. Louis

- ♥ Crystal Cave

- ♥ Dickerson Park Zoo

- ♥ Fantastic Caverns

- ♥ Forest Park

- ♥ Fox Theatre and Tours

- ♥ Gateway Arch & Riverboat Cruises

- ♥ Grand Falls, Joplin

- ♥ Grant's Farm

- ♥ Harry S. Truman Library & Museum
- ♥ Historic St. Charles
- ♥ Hollywood Wax Museum
- ♥ Japanese Stroll Garden, Springfield
- ♥ Jefferson Barracks Historic Park
- ♥ Kansas City Zoo
- ♥ Kemper Museum of Contemporary Art
- ♥ Mark Twain National Forest
- ♥ Marvel Cave
- ♥ Missouri Botanical Garden
- ♥ Muny Theater
- ♥ Nelson-Atkins Museum of Art
- ♥ Old Cathedral
- ♥ Opera Theatre of St. Louis
- ♥ Precious Moments Art Museum
- ♥ Precious Moments Chapel, Carthage
- ♥ Richardson's Candy House, Joplin
- ♥ Ride The Ducks, Branson
- ♥ Ripley's Believe It Or Not Museum
- ♥ Rockcliffe Mansion
- ♥ Runge Conservation Nature Center
- ♥ Saint Louis Art Museum
- ♥ Saint Louis Science Center
- ♥ Science City

- ♥ Shelter Gardens, Columbia
- ♥ Shepherd of the Hills Fish Hatchery Conservation Centre
- ♥ Showboat Branson Belle
- ♥ Silver Dollar City
- ♥ Six Flags
- ♥ Soldiers' Memorial Military Museum
- ♥ Springfield Conservation Nature Center
- ♥ St. Louis Union Station
- ♥ St. Louis Zoo
- ♥ Stone Hill Winery
- ♥ Table Rock State Park
- ♥ The National World War One Museum
- ♥ Toy and Miniature Museum
- ♥ Veterans Memorial Museum
- ♥ Washington Avenue Loft District
- ♥ Wilson's Creek National Battlefield
- ♥ Wolf Sanctuary, Eureka
- ♥ Worlds of Fun, Kansas City

Things To Do In Montana For Couples

Things to do in Montana for couples. Read romantic love poems to your sweetie surrounded by hot springs, watch the sun rise over a lake - a great place for romantic picnic ideas, too.

- ♥ Alberta Bair Theater for Performing Arts
- ♥ Alder Gulch Short Line
- ♥ Alpine Theatre Project

- ♥ Beartooth Scenic Byway
- ♥ Beartooth Wagon & Sleigh Rides
- ♥ Big Sky Scenic Lift
- ♥ Billings Historic Tour
- ♥ Bozeman Hot Springs
- ♥ Conrad Mansion, Kalispell
- ♥ Custer Battlefield Tours
- ♥ Custer Country Southeastern Montana Birding Trail
- ♥ Dave Blackburn's Kootenai Angler, Libby
- ♥ Glacier National Park - St. Mary Lake, Lake McDonald
- ♥ Glacier Sea Kayaking, Whitefish
- ♥ Going-To-The-Sun Road
- ♥ Great Northern Brewing Company
- ♥ Lemhi Pass
- ♥ McGinnis Meadows Cattle Guest Ranch
- ♥ Missoula Valley Birding and Nature Trail
- ♥ Montana Pro Rodeo Hall and Wall of Fame
- ♥ Montana Troutwranglers, Bozeman
- ♥ Moss Mansion, Billings
- ♥ Norris Hot Springs
- ♥ Old Fire Tower (Guardian of the Gulch)
- ♥ Our Lady of the Rockies, Butte
- ♥ Paris Gibson Square Museum of Art
- ♥ Pictograph Cave State Park

♥ Rainbow Carriage Service, Inc., Kalispell

♥ Red Rocks Lake National Wildlife Refuge

♥ Rocking Z Guest Ranch, Wolf Creek

♥ Rocky Mountain Elk Foundation

♥ Seeley-Swan Scenic Drive

♥ Tizer Botanic Gardens and Arboretum

♥ Whoopah Loop Tours by WRC, Billings - Lewis & Clark monument, Little Big Horn

♥ Upper Missouri River Breaks National Monument

♥ Yellowstone National Park - Old Faithful Geyser, Mammoth Hot Springs, Tower Falls, Grand Canyon of the Yellowstone

♥ Zoo Montana

Things To Do In Nebraska For Couples

Things to do in Nebraska for couples. Take romantic pictures by lakes, recite romantic poems to each other by fountains, watch a sunset and sunrise over the water.

♥ Arbor Day Farm, Nebraska City

♥ Arbor Lodge State Historical Park

♥ Bemis Center for Contemporary Arts

♥ Boulder Creek Amusement Park

♥ Chalco Hills Recreation Area

♥ Dobby's Frontier Town, Alliance

♥ Durham Western Heritage Museum

♥ Eugene T. Mahoney State Park

♥ Fisher/Rainbow Fountain, Hastings

♥ Folsom Children's Zoo and Botanical Gardens

- ♥ Fonner Park Thoroughbred Horse Racing
- ♥ Fort Cody Trading Post
- ♥ Fort Sidney Museum and Post
- ♥ Commander's Home
- ♥ Fremont Dinner Train
- ♥ General Crook House Museum
- ♥ Gerald R. Ford Birthsite and Gardens
- ♥ Girls and Boys Town
- ♥ Great Platte River Road Archway Monument
- ♥ Heartland of America Park
- ♥ Henry Doorly Zoo
- ♥ Hyde Observatory
- ♥ Images of Nature, Omaha
- ♥ James Arthur Vineyards
- ♥ Joslyn Art Museum
- ♥ Joslyn Castle
- ♥ Kenefick Park
- ♥ Lee G. Simmons Conservation Park and Wildlife Safari
- ♥ Louis E May Historical Museum, Fremont
- ♥ Mallory Kountze Planetarium
- ♥ Mansion on the Hill, Ogallala
- ♥ Memorial Park, Omaha
- ♥ Merritt Reservoir
- ♥ Offutt Air Force Base

- ♥ Omaha Botanical / Lauritzen Gardens

- ♥ Pioneers Park Nature Center, Lincoln

- ♥ Riverside Zoo

- ♥ Rosenblatt Stadium

- ♥ Smiths Falls State Park

- ♥ Snake River Falls

- ♥ Standing Bear Lake

- ♥ State Capitol

- ♥ Strategic Air and Space Museum

Things To Do In Nevada For Couples

Things to do in Nevada for couples. Nevada vacations offer romantic proposals ideas, weekend getaways and romantic fun.

- ♥ Animal Ark

- ♥ Art Attack Gallery, Incline Village

- ♥ Bartley Ranch Park

- ♥ Bellagio Gallery of Fine Art

- ♥ Best and Belcher Mine Tour

- ♥ Big Bend State Park

- ♥ Black Canyon River Raft Tours, Boulder City

- ♥ Bonnie Springs Ranch Old Nevada Canterbury Wedding Chapel, Las Vegas

- ♥ Chollar Mine

- ♥ Circus Circus Adventuredome Theme Park

- ♥ Del Rio Cruises, Laughlin

- ♥ Eiffel Tower

- ♥ Fleischmann Planetarium
- ♥ Floyd Lamb State Park
- ♥ Fountains at Bellagio
- ♥ Fourth Ward School Museum
- ♥ Fremont Street Experience
- ♥ Gondola Rides at the Venetian
- ♥ Governor's Mansion, Carson City
- ♥ Great Basin Adventure, Reno
- ♥ Grimes Point/Hidden Cave Archaeological Site
- ♥ Heavenly Aerial Tram, South Lake Tahoe
- ♥ Hoover Dam
- ♥ Imperial Palace Auto Collection
- ♥ King Tut's Tomb & Museum
- ♥ Lake Mead Cruises
- ♥ Las Vegas Motor Speedway
- ♥ Las Vegas Natural History Museum
- ♥ Liberace Museum
- ♥ Lion Habitat @ The MGM Grand Hotel & Casino
- ♥ Little Chapel of the Flowers, Las Vegas
- ♥ M.S. Dixie II, Sunnyside Tahoe City - dinner cruises
- ♥ Mills Park Railroad
- ♥ National Automobile Museum
- ♥ Neon Museum
- ♥ Ponderosa Ranch, Incline Village

♥ Rancho San Rafael Park

♥ Red Rock Canyon National Conservation Area

♥ Reno Arch

♥ Reno-Tahoe Sky Tours

♥ Sand Harbor

♥ Shark Reef

♥ Sparks Marina Park

♥ Spooner Lake Cross Country Ski Area

♥ St. Mary in the Mountains Catholic Church, VA city

♥ Sundance Helicopters, Las Vegas

♥ U.S.S. Riverside, Laughlin

♥ Valley of Fire State Park, Overton

♥ Virginia and Truckee Railroad

♥ Virginia City

♥ Wingfield Park Amphitheater

New Hampshire Attractions For Couples

New Hampshire attractions for couples to see together. Write your own romantic stories, think romantic thoughts, and spend time with the one you love.

♥ Canterbury Shaker Village, Henniker

♥ Captain Bill's Charters - deep sea fishing, scuba diving

♥ Cathedral of the Pines, Jaffrey

♥ Conway Scenic Railroad

♥ Gilman Garrison House

♥ Governor John Langdon House

♥ Iron Furnace Interpretive Center

♥ Isles of Shoals Steamship Company, Portsmouth - whale watches, lighthouse cruises, sunset dinner cruises

♥ Jackson House

♥ Jaffrey Speedway & Hobby Slot Car Racing

♥ John Paul Jones House

♥ King Pine Ski Area

♥ Littleton Coin Company

♥ Littleton Grist Mill

♥ Moffat-Ladd House And Garden

♥ Mount Washington Cruises - Scenic cruises, dinner dances

♥ New Hampshire International Speedway

♥ Pat's Peak Ski Area

♥ Pierce Manse, Concord

♥ Portsmouth Harbor Light House

♥ Prescott Park Arts Festival

♥ Rocky Ridge Ranch, Littleton

♥ Seacoast Repertory Theatre

♥ Squam Lake Tours

♥ Storrs Pond Recreation Area

♥ Warner House

♥ Wentworth-Gardner House, Portsmouth

♥ What's Up Ballooning - balloon ride over Contoocook River Valley

New Jersey Attractions For Couples

These New Jersey attractions for couples to see include walks on New Jersey beaches and other romantic things to do.

♥ Acorn Hall, Morristown

♥ Atlantic City - casinos & boardwalk

♥ Bayside Center

♥ Belmar Beach and Boardwalk

♥ Cape May Bird Observatory

♥ Cape May County Dinner Cruise

♥ Cape May Stage

♥ Casino Pier & Waterworks, Seaside Heights

♥ Cattus Island County Park

♥ Cohanzick Zoo

♥ Deep Cut Gardens, Middletown

♥ Four Sisters Winery, Hackettstown

♥ Ghost Tour of Ocean City

♥ Grounds for Sculpture, Princeton

♥ Historic Morven

♥ Lakewood BlueClaws

♥ Lincoln Park Historic District, Newark

♥ Jenkinson's Pavillion Boardwalk and Amusement Park

♥ McCarter Theatre Center for the Performing Arts

♥ Morey's Piers

♥ Nature Center of Cape May

♥ New Jersey Symphony Orchestra, Newark

♥ Northlandz, Flemington

♥ Off Broad Street Players, Bridgeton

♥ Potter's Tavern, Bridgeton

♥ Princeton Battlefield State Park

♥ Rainbow III Deep Sea Fishing, Ocean City

♥ Ridge Light Opera

♥ Rockingham Historic Site

♥ Saint Ann's Roman Catholic Church, Wildwood

♥ Schuyler Hamilton House

♥ Shakespeare Garden - on the campus of the College of Saint Elizabeth

♥ ShowPlace Ice Cream Parlor, Beach Haven

♥ Surflight Theatre

♥ Trenton Battle Monument

♥ Turkey Swamp Park

♥ Unionville Vineyards

♥ Wick House Herb Garden

♥ Wildwood

Things To Do In New Mexico For Couples

These New Mexico attractions include romantic travel ideas to all parts of the state. Romance abounds with things to do with your soulmate.

♥ Albuquerque Aquarium

♥ Albuquerque Biological Park

♥ Albuquerque Museum

♥ American International Rattlesnake Museum

- ♥ ArtsCrawl
- ♥ Bataan Memorial Military Museum & Library
- ♥ Bitter Lake National Wildlife Refuge
- ♥ Bonito Lake
- ♥ Canyon Road, Santa Fe
- ♥ Carlsbad Caverns National Park
- ♥ Carlsbad Cruise Lines - sunset dinner cruise
- ♥ Casa Rondena Winery
- ♥ Christmas On The Pecos River
- ♥ City of Rocks State Park
- ♥ Cliff's Amusement Park
- ♥ Cross of the Martyrs
- ♥ El Rancho de las Golondrinas
- ♥ Georgia O'Keeffe Museum
- ♥ Gruet Winery
- ♥ Hillcrest Park Zoo
- ♥ Indian Pueblo Culture Center
- ♥ Institute of American Indian Arts Museum
- ♥ Kokopelli Rafting Adventures
- ♥ Lewallen Contemporary Art
- ♥ Living Desert State Park
- ♥ LodeStar Astronomy Center
- ♥ Loretto Chapel
- ♥ Luz Trail

- ♥ Madison Vineyards and Winery

- ♥ Maxwell Museum of Anthropology

- ♥ Museum of Fine Arts

- ♥ Museum of International Folk Art

- ♥ National Hispanic Cultural Center of New Mexico

- ♥ New Mexico Museum of Natural History & Science

- ♥ New Mexico State Capitol

- ♥ Old Town, Albuquerque

- ♥ Oliver Lee Memorial State Park

- ♥ Palace of the Governors

- ♥ Petroglyph National Monument

- ♥ Pistachio Tree Ranch

- ♥ Pueblo de Taos

- ♥ Pueblo of Santa Anna

- ♥ Putt-Putt Golf & Games, Albuquerque

- ♥ Rainbow Ryders, Inc - hot air balloon rides

- ♥ Red River Ski and Snowboard Area

- ♥ Rio Grande Botanic Garden

- ♥ Rio Grande Nature Center

- ♥ Rio Grande Zoological Park

- ♥ Ruidoso Downs

- ♥ San Miguel Mission

- ♥ Santa Fe Plaza

- ♥ Santa Fe Southern Railway

♥ Sherwoods Spirit of America

♥ St. Francis Cathedral, Santa Fe

♥ Stahmann Farms, Las Cruces - for pecan lovers

♥ Taos Native Sons Adventures - bike, rafting and snowmobile tours

♥ Taos Ski Valley

♥ Toy Train Depot, Alamogordo

♥ Wheelwright Museum of the American Indian

New York Attractions For Couples

These New York attractions offer romantic Valentine ideas, romantic weekend ideas and lots of fun and togetherness for couples.

♥ Albright Knox Art Gallery, Buffalo

♥ Animal Farm Petting Zoo, Long Island

♥ Aquarium of Niagara

♥ Artpark, Niagara

♥ Battery Park

♥ Botanical Gardens, Buffalo

♥ Bronx Zoo

♥ Brooklyn Bridge

♥ Bryant Park

♥ Buffalo & Erie County Historical Society

♥ Buffalo & Erie County Naval & Military Park

♥ Buffalo Fire Historical Museum

♥ Bully Hill Vineyards, Hammondsport

♥ Captain Bill's Seneca Lake Cruises, Watkins Glen

- ♥ Captain J.P. Cruise Line, Troy - dinner cruise by the Hudson
- ♥ Carnegie Hall
- ♥ Cave of the Winds, Niagara Falls
- ♥ Central Park
- ♥ Chinatown
- ♥ Chrysler Building
- ♥ Coney Island
- ♥ Darien Lake Theme Park & Resort
- ♥ Double M Professional Rodeo, Ballston Spa
- ♥ Ellis Island Immigration Museum
- ♥ Empire State Building
- ♥ Farm Sanctuary, Watkins Glen
- ♥ Fashion Institute of Technology
- ♥ Flatiron Building
- ♥ Forbes Magazine Gallery
- ♥ Fountain Plaza, Buffalo
- ♥ Frank Lloyd Wright's Darwin D Martin House
- ♥ Frick Collection
- ♥ Greenwich Village
- ♥ Hayden Planetarium
- ♥ House of Frankenstein Wax Museum, Lake George
- ♥ Hyde Hall, Cooperstown
- ♥ Keuka Spring Vineyards, Penn Yan
- ♥ Lake George Shoreline Cruise

- ♥ Lake Otsego Boat Tours
- ♥ Lark Street Neighborhood, Albany
- ♥ Little Italy
- ♥ Lockport Locks & Erie Canal Cruises
- ♥ Lucy-Desi Museum
- ♥ Madison Square Garden
- ♥ Majestic Theatre
- ♥ Maid of the Mist & Niagara Falls
- ♥ Metropolitan Museum of Art
- ♥ Millard Fillmore Museum
- ♥ Miss Buffalo Cruises
- ♥ Museum of Modern Art
- ♥ National Baseball Hall of Fame and Museum
- ♥ National Shrine Basilica of Our Lady of Fatima, Youngstown
- ♥ New York Aquarium
- ♥ New York Waterways Sightseeing Cruises
- ♥ New York Yankees & Yankee Stadium
- ♥ Niagara Falls State Park
- ♥ Old Fort Niagara
- ♥ Our Lady Of Lourdes Grotto
- ♥ Our Lady of Victory Basilica and National Shrine, Lackawanna
- ♥ Parasailing Adventures, Lake George
- ♥ Peconic River Herb Farm
- ♥ Quogue Wildlife Refuge

- ♥ Rainbow Air, Inc - helicopter tour of Niagara Falls
- ♥ Riverbank State Park
- ♥ Robert H. Treman State Park
- ♥ Rockefeller Center
- ♥ Roosevelt Island Aerial Tram
- ♥ Rubin Museum of Art
- ♥ Sapsucker Woods Sanctuary
- ♥ Saranac Brewery Tour Center, Utica
- ♥ Seneca Lake State Park
- ♥ Seneca Park Zoo
- ♥ Sony Wonder Technology Lab
- ♥ South Street Seaport
- ♥ St Joseph's Cathedral, Buffalo
- ♥ St. Patrick's Cathedral - beautiful place to recite romantic wedding vows
- ♥ St. Paul's Chapel, NYC
- ♥ Staten Island Ferry
- ♥ Statue of Liberty
- ♥ Tickner's Canoes, Old Forge - go kayaking
- ♥ Times Square Top of the Rock
- ♥ Uncle Sam Boat Tours, Alexandria Bay - lunch and dinner cruises
- ♥ Union Square
- ♥ United Nations HQ
- ♥ Wall Street
- ♥ Whirlpool State Park

♥ Wilcox Mansion, Buffalo

♥ Yaddo Gardens, Saratoga Springs

North Carolina Things To Do

These North Carolina things to do for couples offer unique date ideas, Valentine day ideas and inexpensive romantic ideas.

♥ 30 Acres and a Mule Farm, Jacksonville

♥ Artspace, Raleigh

♥ Ashe County Cheese Company

♥ Asheville Tourists Minor League Baseball Team

♥ Barn Dinner Theatre, Greensboro

♥ Battleship North Carolina, Wilmington

♥ Biltmore Estate

♥ Blandwood Mansion, Greensboro

♥ Blue Ridge Parkway, Asheville

♥ Bodie Island Lighthouse

♥ Bog Garden, Greensboro

♥ Bur-Mil Park

♥ Cape Hatteras Lighthouse

♥ Cape Hatteras National Seashore

♥ Carolina Nights Dinner Theater, Maggie Valley

♥ Castle McCulloch

♥ Charlotte Museum of History

♥ Chatham Hill Winery

♥ Cherokee Visitors Center

♥ Chunky Gal Stables, Franklin - guided horseback rides

♥ Colburn Earth Science Museum

♥ Cooper Creek Trout Farm

♥ Corolla Outback Adventures, Outer Banks - ATV tours to North Beach, wild horse tours, kayaking

♥ Discovery Place, Charlotte

♥ Duke University Chapel

♥ Edge of the World, Banner Elk - climb, canoe or raft

♥ Elizabethan Gardens, Manteo

♥ Fort Macon State Park

♥ Grandfather Mountain

♥ Historic Oakwood, Raleigh

♥ Historic Rosedale

♥ Jambbas Ranch, Fayetteville

♥ J.C. Raulston Arboretum

♥ Kitty Hawk

♥ Korner's Folly, Kernersville

♥ Latimer House, Wilmington

♥ Linville Caverns

♥ Mason Mountain Mine and Cowee Gift Shop

♥ Mason's Ruby & Sapphire Mine

♥ McDowell Nature Center and Preserve

♥ Mint Museum of Art, Charlotte

♥ Morehead Planetarium

- ♥ Nags Head
- ♥ Nantahala Outdoor Center
- ♥ NC Zoo
- ♥ New Hanover County Arboretum
- ♥ North Carolina Aquarium at Fort Fisher
- ♥ North Carolina Aquarium on Roanoke Island
- ♥ North Carolina Museum of Art
- ♥ North Carolina Museum of Life and Science
- ♥ North Carolina Museum of Natural Sciences
- ♥ North Carolina Zoological Park
- ♥ Old Cardinal Gem Mine & Gift Shop
- ♥ Old Salem
- ♥ Paramount's Carowinds
- ♥ Pea Island National Wildlife Refuge
- ♥ Red Oak Brewery
- ♥ River Park North, Greenville
- ♥ Rolling Thunder River Company, Bryson City - whitewater rafting
- ♥ Rose Creek Mine Rock & Gift Shop
- ♥ Sarah P. Duke Gardens
- ♥ Shelley Lake Park
- ♥ Sliding Rock, Brevard
- ♥ Soco Gardens Zoo
- ♥ Southern Highland Folk Art Center
- ♥ Stevens Center, Winston Salem

♥ Stompin' Ground, Maggie Valley

♥ Thalian Hall Center for the Performing Arts

♥ Tryon Palace Historic Sites and Gardens, New Bern

♥ UNC Charlotte Botanical Gardens

♥ Weymouth Woods Sandhills Nature Preserve

♥ William B. Umstead State Park

♥ Wilmington Sharks

♥ Wilson Rose Garden

North Dakota Attractions For Couples

These North Dakota attractions offer couples Valentines day ideas and places and ways to propose to your soulmate.

♥ Bismarck Bobcats

♥ Bottineau Winter Park

♥ Camp Hancock State Historic Site

♥ Celebrity Walk of Fame

♥ Cross Ranch State Park

♥ Dakota Zoo

♥ Double Ditch Indian Village State Historic Site

♥ Fargo Moorhead Community Theatre

♥ Fargo Moorhead Red Hawks

♥ Fargo Theatre

♥ Fargodome

♥ Fort Abraham Lincoln State Park

♥ Geographical Center of North America Monument, Bottineau

♥ Greater Grand Forks Symphony Orchestra

♥ Lake Metigoshe State Park

♥ Lewis and Clark State Park

♥ Little Missouri State Park

♥ Maple River Winery, Casselton

♥ Niewoehner Bell Tower, Bottineau

♥ North Dakota State Fair, Minot

♥ North Dakota State Capitol Building

♥ Pierre Bottineau Statue

♥ Putnam House, Carrington

♥ Ralph Engelstad Arena

♥ Red River State Recreation Area

♥ Red River Zoo

♥ Roosevelt Park Zoo

♥ Saint-Germain l'Auxerrois

♥ Siouxland Buffalo Ranch

♥ St Michael's Catholic Church, Grand Forks

♥ Turtle River State Park

♥ Wheat Monument, Williston

♥ World's Largest Buffalo Monument, Jamestown

Things To Do In Ohio For Couples

These things to do in Ohio for couples offer Valentines day ideas for boyfriend or girlfriend, romantic weekend getaways or fun one day romance escapes.

♥ Adventure Cove, Wilmington

- ♥ African Safari Wildlife Park, Port Clinton
- ♥ Akron Civic Theater
- ♥ Beach Waterpark, Lebanon
- ♥ Beaver Creek State Park
- ♥ Brumbaugh Fruit Farm, Greenville
- ♥ Bull's Run Nature Sanctuary and Arboretum
- ♥ Carousel Dinner Theater, Akron
- ♥ Carriage Hill MetroPark & Farm, Dayton
- ♥ Cedar Point
- ♥ Cincinnati Horticultural Society
- ♥ Cincinnati Nature Center
- ♥ Cincinnati Zoo & Botanical Gardens
- ♥ Cleveland Botanical Garden
- ♥ Columbus Crew
- ♥ Columbus Symphony Orchestra
- ♥ Columbus Zoo & Aquarium
- ♥ Deerassic Park Education Center, Cambridge
- ♥ E.L.H.S. Alumni Clock Tower, East Liverpool
- ♥ Firelands Winery
- ♥ Franklin Park Conservatory, Columbus
- ♥ Geauga Lake
- ♥ Georgetown Vineyards
- ♥ Ghostly Manor, Sandusky
- ♥ Glacial Grooves, Sandusky

- ♥ Harry London Candies, North Canton
- ♥ Historic Roscoe Village, Columbus
- ♥ Hower House, Akron
- ♥ Huron Playhouse
- ♥ Krohn Conservatory
- ♥ Lyman Harbor, Sandusky
- ♥ Meier's Wine Cellars
- ♥ Mon Ami Historic Winery and Restaurant
- ♥ Newport Aquarium
- ♥ Paramount's Kings Island
- ♥ Perry's Cave, Sandusky
- ♥ Pro Football Hall of Fame, Canton
- ♥ River Downs Racetrack
- ♥ RiverScape MetroPark, Dayton
- ♥ Rock & Roll Hall of Fame & Museum
- ♥ Salt Fork State Park
- ♥ Schiller Park, Columbus
- ♥ Schrock's Amish Farm, Columbus
- ♥ Schultz Mansion, Zanesville
- ♥ Showboat Majestic, Cincinnati
- ♥ Six Flags World of Adventure
- ♥ Stan Hywet Hall and Gardens
- ♥ The Akron Zoo
- ♥ Virginia Kendall Park, Akron

♥ William Howard Taft National Historic Site

Things To Do In Oklahoma For Couples

Things to do in Oklahoma for couples. If you're looking for Valentines day romance or adult romance ideas to share with your sweetie, check out our ideas.

♥ 45th Infantry Division Museum

♥ AT&T Bricktown Ballpark

♥ Bricktown Canal

♥ Festival of the Arts, Oklahoma City

♥ Frank Phillips Home, Bartlesville

♥ Gilcrease Museum, Tulsa

♥ Harn Homestead

♥ Hefner Lake & Park

♥ International Gymnastics Hall of Fame

♥ M.A. Doran Gallery

♥ Marland Estate Mansion, Ponca City

♥ Martin Park Nature Center

♥ Myriad Botanical Gardens

♥ National Cowboy and Western Heritage Museum

♥ National Softball Hall of Fame

♥ Oklahoma Aquarium

♥ Oklahoma City Art Museum

♥ Oklahoma City National Memorial

♥ Oklahoma City Zoo

♥ Oklahoma Firefighters Museum

- ♥ Oklahoma Gardening Studio Grounds, Stillwater
- ♥ Oklahoma Heritage Center
- ♥ Oklahoma Jazz Hall of Fame
- ♥ Omniplex
- ♥ Oral Roberts University
- ♥ Overholser Mansion
- ♥ Philbrook Museum of Art
- ♥ Pittsburg County Genealogical & Historical Society
- ♥ Price Tower Arts Center, Bartlesville
- ♥ Remington Park
- ♥ River Parks, Tulsa
- ♥ Safaris Exotic Wildlife Sanctuary
- ♥ Sam Noble Oklahoma Museum of Natural History
- ♥ The Pumpkin Patch, Bartlesville
- ♥ Thomas Foreman Historic Home, Muskogee
- ♥ Tucker Tower, Ardmore
- ♥ Tulsa Air and Space Museum
- ♥ Tulsa Garden Center
- ♥ Tulsa Zoo and Living Museum
- ♥ Water Taxi of Oklahoma
- ♥ Woolaroc Ranch, Museum & Wildlife Preserve

Things To Do In Oregon For Couples

These things to do in Oregon offer couples adult romance ideas and cheap and fun date ideas.

- ♥ A.C. Gilbert's Discovery Village, Salem

- ♥ Beverly Cleary Sculptures At Grant Park

- ♥ Captain George Flavel House Museum, Astoria

- ♥ Classical Chinese Garden, Portland

- ♥ Coaster Theater Playhouse, Cannon Beach

- ♥ Columbia River Gorge - Mount Hood Loop

- ♥ Columbia River Maritime Museum

- ♥ Ecola State Park

- ♥ End of the Oregon Trail Interpretive Center

- ♥ Evergreen Aviation Museum, McMinnville

- ♥ Harris Beach State Park

- ♥ Heceta Head State Park

- ♥ Helvetia Vineyards & Winery

- ♥ Hendricks Park, Eugene

- ♥ HillCrest Vineyard, Roseburg

- ♥ International Rose Test Garden

- ♥ Ira Keller - Forecourt Fountain

- ♥ Japanese Garden

- ♥ Jerry's Rogue Jets, Gold Beach - jet boat tours

- ♥ Jessie M. Honeyman Memorial State Park

- ♥ Joseph Wood Hill Park

- ♥ King Estate, Eugene

- ♥ Lakeside Gardens

- ♥ Macleay Park

- ♥ Mail Boat Hydro-Jet Trips, Gold Beach
- ♥ Marine Discovery Tours, Newport - sea life cruise
- ♥ Mount Hood
- ♥ Mount Tabor Park
- ♥ Multnomah Falls
- ♥ Noah's River Adventure, Ashland - rafting, fishing
- ♥ Oregon Cabaret Theatre
- ♥ Oregon Coast Aquarium
- ♥ Oregon Maritime Center and Museum
- ♥ Oregon Museum of Science and Industry
- ♥ Oregon Shakespeare Festival
- ♥ Oregon Zoo
- ♥ Owen Memorial Rose Garden
- ♥ Pioneer Courthouse, Portland
- ♥ Pittock Mansion
- ♥ Prehistoric Gardens, Gold Beach
- ♥ Rogue Klamath River Adventures
- ♥ Salem's Riverfront Carousel
- ♥ Salmon Street Springs
- ♥ Schreiner's Iris Gardens
- ♥ Sea Lion Caves
- ♥ Seaside
- ♥ Sheriff John's Classic Cars, Gold Beach
- ♥ Silvan Ridge-Hinman Vineyards

♥ Tillamook Cheese Factory

♥ Tom McCall Waterfront Park

♥ Vietnam Veterans of Oregon Memorial

♥ Washington Park, Portland

♥ Westmoreland Park

♥ Yaquina Bay Lighthouse

Things To Do In Pennsylvania For Couples

Things to do in Pennsylvania for couples offer cheap date ideas and creative romantic ideas.

♥ Academy of Natural Sciences, Philly

♥ American Music Theater, Lancaster

♥ Andy Warhol Museum

♥ Benjamin Franklin National Memorial

♥ Betsy Ross House

♥ Bowman's Hill Wildflower Preserve, Doylestown

♥ Carnegie Museum of Art

♥ Carnegie Museum of Natural History

♥ Carnegie Science Center

♥ Cathedral Basilica of Saints Peter and Paul, Philly

♥ Codorus State Park, Hanover

♥ Congress Hall

♥ Dutch Apple Dinner Theatre, Lancaster

♥ Dutch Wonderland Family Amusement Park

♥ Edgar Allan Poe House

- ♥ Erie Land Lighthouse

- ♥ Eye Catcher Charters, Erie - fishing

- ♥ Farnsworth House Candlelight Ghost Walks, Gettysburg

- ♥ Fonthill Museum, Doylestown

- ♥ Fort Hunter Mansion and Park, Harrisburg

- ♥ Fort Pitt Museum and Blockhouse

- ♥ Franklin Court

- ♥ Franklin Institute

- ♥ Frick Art Museum

- ♥ Fulton Opera House, Lancaster

- ♥ Gateway Clipper Fleet, Pittsburgh

- ♥ Gettysburg Battlefield Tours

- ♥ Gettysburg National Military Park

- ♥ Ghost Tour Of Philadelphia

- ♥ Grand Canyon of Pennsylvania

- ♥ Harley-Davidson Motor Co. Final Assembly Museum, York

- ♥ Hartwood, Pittsburgh

- ♥ Hershey's Chocolate World

- ♥ Hershey Gardens

- ♥ HersheyPark

- ♥ Hershey Trolley Works

- ♥ Hiawatha Riverboat, Susquehanna State Park - cruise

- ♥ Horseshoe Curve National Historic Landmark

- ♥ Independence Hall

- ♥ Independence Seaport Museum

- ♥ Indian Echo Caverns, Hershey

- ♥ Jim Thorpe River Adventures - rafting, kayaking

- ♥ Johnstown Flood National Memorial

- ♥ Johnstown Inclined Plane

- ♥ Kennywood Amusement Park

- ♥ Lackawanna Coal Mine Tour, Scranton

- ♥ Lake Tobias Wildlife Park

- ♥ Land of Little Horses

- ♥ Liberty Bell

- ♥ Liberty Museum

- ♥ Lights of Liberty

- ♥ Lincoln Caverns and Whisper Rocks, Huntingdon

- ♥ Longwood Gardens, Kennett Square

- ♥ Love Park, Philly

- ♥ Mazza Vineyards, Erie

- ♥ Memorial Hall, Philly

- ♥ Montage Mountain, Scranton

- ♥ National Apple Harvest Festival, Gettysburg

- ♥ National Shrine of Our Lady of Czestochowa, Doylestown

- ♥ National Shrine of St. John Neumann

- ♥ Nissley Vineyards & Winery Estate, Lancaster

- ♥ Old City Hall, Philly

- ♥ Pennsylvania Renaissance Fair, Manheim

- ♥ Philadelphia Museum of Art

- ♥ Philadelphia Vietnam Veterans Memorial

- ♥ Philadelphia Zoo

- ♥ Phipps Conservatory and Botanical Gardens

- ♥ Pinnacle Ridge Winery

- ♥ PNC Park

- ♥ Point State Park, Pittsburgh

- ♥ Presque Isle State Park

- ♥ QVC Studio Tour, West Chester

- ♥ Railroaders Museum, Altoona

- ♥ Rittenhouse Square

- ♥ Rodin Museum

- ♥ St. Anthony's Chapel, Pittsburgh

- ♥ Steamtown National Historic Site, Scranton

- ♥ Straub Brewery

- ♥ Tioga Central Railroad, Wellsboro

- ♥ Tomb of the Unknown Soldier, Philly

- ♥ United States Mint

- ♥ University of Pennsylvania Museum of Archaeology and Anthropology

- ♥ Waldameer & Water World

- ♥ William Brinton 1704 House and Historic Site

Rhode Island Attractions For Couples

These Rhode Island attractions offer couples free date ideas and romantic evening date ideas. Hand your sweetie some free love coupons for places to see throughout the state.

- ♥ Bank of America City Center
- ♥ Bannister's Wharf
- ♥ Beavertail Lighthouse
- ♥ Bird's Eye View Helicopters, Middletown - take a tour
- ♥ Blithewold Mansion, Gardens and Arboretum
- ♥ Brenton Point State Park
- ♥ Brown University
- ♥ Butterfly Zoo, Tiverton
- ♥ Chateau-sur-Mer
- ♥ Culinary Archives & Museum At Johnson & Wales University
- ♥ Fall Foliage Automobile Tours, Pawtucket
- ♥ Fort Barton
- ♥ Fort Wetherill State Park
- ♥ Governor Henry Lippitt House Museum
- ♥ Green Animals Topiary Garden
- ♥ Greenvale Vineyards, Portsmouth
- ♥ International Tennis Hall of Fame
- ♥ John Brown House Museum
- ♥ Linden Place, Bristol
- ♥ Manisses Animal Farm, Block Island
- ♥ Narragansett Bay National Estuarine Sanctuary
- ♥ Newport Art Museum
- ♥ Newport Historical Society Walking Tours
- ♥ Newport Vineyards & Winery

- ♥ Norman Bird Sanctuary

- ♥ Prospect Terrace Park

- ♥ Roger Williams Park & Zoo

- ♥ Sachuset Beach

- ♥ Sachuest Point National Wildlife Refuge

- ♥ Sachuest Wildlife Park

- ♥ Sakonnet Vineyards

- ♥ Salve Regina University

- ♥ Secret Garden Walking Tour, Newport

- ♥ Seal Watches to Rose Island Lighthouse, Newport

- ♥ Slater Memorial Park

- ♥ Slater Mill Historic Site

- ♥ Smith's Castle, North Kingstown

- ♥ Stadium Theatre, Woonsocket

- ♥ The RISD Museum

- ♥ Tiverton Four Corners

South Carolina Attractions For Couples

These South Carolina attractions offer couples fun and sun on South Carolina beaches and fun date ideas.

- ♥ Ace Basin Tours

- ♥ Adventure Carolina, Columbia - canoe and kayak tours

- ♥ Aiken-Rhett House

- ♥ Alligator Adventure

- ♥ Ashtabula Plantation

♥ Beachwalker County Park, Kiawah Island

♥ BMW Zentrum and Gallery

♥ Brookgreen Gardens

♥ Build-A-Bear Workshop, Myrtle Beach

♥ Cap'n Rod's Lowcountry Plantation Tours, Georgetown

♥ Carolina Ballet Theatre

♥ Carolina Buggy Tours, Beaufort

♥ Carolina Safari Jeep Tours, Myrtle Beach

♥ Centre Stage, Greenville's Professional Theater

♥ Charleston's Pirates & Buccaneers

♥ Charleston Tea Plantation

♥ Charleston Waterfront Park

♥ Cheraw State Park

♥ Cherry Grove Fishing Pier

♥ Citadel Archives & Museum

♥ Civil War Walk, Charleston

♥ Classic Carriage Tours, Charleston

♥ Downtown Marina Of Beaufort

♥ Drayton Hall

♥ Edisto Island Serpentarium

♥ Edisto Memorial Gardens

♥ Fort Moultrie National Monument

♥ Fort Sumter National Monument

♥ Greenville Zoo

- ♥ Gullah Heritage Trail Tours, Hilton Head Island
- ♥ Hagood Mill, Pickens
- ♥ Harbour Town Lighthouse, Hilton Head
- ♥ Hatcher Garden and Woodland Preserve, Spartanburg
- ♥ Historic Homes Walk, Charleston
- ♥ Huntington Beach State Park
- ♥ Kaminski House Museum
- ♥ Kensington Mansion, Columbia
- ♥ Kilgore-Lewis House, Greenville
- ♥ Lake Marion & Lake Moultrie
- ♥ Magnolia Plantation and Gardens, Charleston
- ♥ Myrtle Beach Pelicans
- ♥ Outside Hilton Head - kayak tours
- ♥ Paris Mountain State Park
- ♥ Reedy River Falls Historic Park & Falls Cottage
- ♥ Rice Museum
- ♥ Ripley's Aquarium
- ♥ Riverbanks Zoo and Botanical Garden
- ♥ Santee State Park
- ♥ Sea Island Plantation Overview
- ♥ Sesquicentennial State Park
- ♥ South Carolina State Fair
- ♥ Spartanburg Little Theatre
- ♥ Spirit of Carolina Dinner Cruise

♥ Swan Lake Iris Garden, Sumter

♥ Table Rock State Park

♥ The Franklin G. Burroughs, Simeon B. Chapin Art Museum

♥ USC Horseshoe

♥ Wallace Sailing Charters, Georgetown

♥ Walnut Grove Plantation, Spartanburg

South Dakota Attractions For Couples

South Dakota attractions for couples to see when on their romantic South Dakota vacations. Enjoy fun romantic ideas, romantic evening ideas and more.

♥ Attraction Tours of the Black Hills

♥ Badlands

♥ Beautiful Rushmore Cave

♥ Black Hills Autumn Expedition

♥ Black Hills Caverns

♥ Black Hills Putt-4-Fun

♥ Black Hills Wild Horse Sanctuary

♥ Central States Fair

♥ Cosmos of the Black Hills

♥ Crazy Horse Memorial and Museum

♥ Crystal Cave Park

♥ Custer State Park

♥ Deadwood & Spearfish Canyon

♥ Deer Mountain

♥ Great Plains Zoo

- ♥ Holy SmokeTrail Rides, Rapid City

- ♥ Homestake Visitors Center

- ♥ Mammoth Site, Hot Springs

- ♥ Mount Rushmore

- ♥ Prehistoric Indian Village, Mitchell

- ♥ Rockin R Rides, Inc., Custer - trail rides, wagon rides

- ♥ Rushmore Tramway

- ♥ South Dakota Acoustic Christmas

- ♥ Stavkirke Chapel in the Hills

- ♥ Storybook Island, Rapid City

- ♥ Terry Peak, Lead

- ♥ Wildcat Valley Sanctuary of the Black Hills, Keystone

Things To Do In Tennessee For Couples

These things to do in Tennessee offer couples good date ideas and honeymoon ideas.

- ♥ Adventure Science Center

- ♥ Athena's Statue

- ♥ Bays Mountain Park & Planetarium

- ♥ Beachaven Vineyards & Winery

- ♥ Belle Meade Plantation

- ♥ Bluff Mountain Adventures, Sevierville - ATV tours

- ♥ Bluff View Art District

- ♥ Bristol Caverns

- ♥ Cane Creek State Park

- ♥ Carnton Plantation
- ♥ Chattanooga Ducks
- ♥ Cheekwood Botanical Garden
- ♥ Christmas Village, Nashville
- ♥ Comedy Barn Theater, Pigeon Forge
- ♥ Concord Park, Nashville
- ♥ Coolidge Park
- ♥ Cotton Exchange Building
- ♥ Country Music Hall of Fame and Museum
- ♥ Dickson Gallery of Fine Art, Jackson
- ♥ Dixie Stampede Dinner & Show
- ♥ Dollywood
- ♥ Flyaway Indoor Skydiving, Pigeon Forge
- ♥ Forbidden Caverns, Sevierville
- ♥ Gatlinburg Sky Lift
- ♥ Graceland
- ♥ Grand Ole Opry Museum
- ♥ Great Smoky Mountains National Park
- ♥ Hermitage, Home of President Andrew Jackson
- ♥ House Mountain, Knoxville
- ♥ Hunter Museum of American Art
- ♥ Loretta Lynn's Ranch
- ♥ Lost Sea, Sweetwater
- ♥ Marrowbone Lake

- ♥ Memories Theatre

- ♥ Memphis Botanic Garden

- ♥ Memphis Zoo and Aquarium

- ♥ Morris Winery and Vineyard

- ♥ Mysterious Mansion of Gatlinburg

- ♥ NashTrash Tours

- ♥ Nashville War Memorial Auditorium

- ♥ Nashville Zoo at Grassmere

- ♥ National Civil Rights Museum

- ♥ Opryland Hotel Indoor Garden and Collections

- ♥ Parthenon

- ♥ Pigeon Forge Gem Mine

- ♥ Pigeon Forge Super Speedway

- ♥ Pink Palace Museum

- ♥ Point Park and Ochs Museum

- ♥ Ride the Ducks, Memphis

- ♥ Ripley's Haunted Adventure, Gatlinburg

- ♥ Rock and Soul Museum

- ♥ Rock City Gardens, Lookout Mountain

- ♥ Ruby Falls

- ♥ Scenic Helicopter Tours - Smokies tour

- ♥ Smoky Mountain Jubilee

- ♥ Smoky Mountain Winery

- ♥ Southern Belle Riverboat, Chattanooga - dinner cruise

♥ Sun Studio, Memphis

♥ Sweet Fanny Adams Theatre & Music Hall

♥ Tennessee Aquarium

♥ Tennessee State Museum

♥ The Houston Museum of Decorative Arts

♥ Travellers Rest Historic House Museum

♥ Tuckaleechee Caverns, Inc.

♥ Walnut Street Bridge, Chattanooga

♥ Warner Park Zoo

♥ Willow Springs Park

Things To Do In Texas For Couples

These things to do in Texas offer couples ideas for a fun date and ideas for a romantic night together.

♥ Abilene Zoo

♥ Alamo

♥ Austin Duck Adventures

♥ Austin Segway Tour

♥ Barton Springs Pool, Austin

♥ Bayou Bend, Houston

♥ Bayou Wildlife Park

♥ Bishop's Palace, Galveston

♥ Buckhorn Saloon and Museum, San Antonio

♥ Burger's Lake

♥ Caprock Canyons State Park

- ♥ Connemara Conservancy
- ♥ Cowtown Coliseum
- ♥ Dallas Arboretum
- ♥ Dallas Museum of Art
- ♥ Dallas World Aquarium
- ♥ Dallas Zoo
- ♥ Enchanted Rock State Natural Area
- ♥ Forest Park Miniature Train
- ♥ Fort Sam Houston Quadrangle
- ♥ Fort Worth Botanical Gardens
- ♥ Fort Worth Museum of Science and History
- ♥ Fort Worth Nature Center & Wildlife Refuge
- ♥ Goliad State Historical Park
- ♥ Houston Museum of Natural Science
- ♥ Houston Zoo
- ♥ Japanese Tea Gardens
- ♥ Kimbell Art Museum
- ♥ Landa Park, New Braunfels
- ♥ Legends of the Game Baseball Museum
- ♥ Log Cabin Village, Fort Worth
- ♥ Lone Star Flight Museum
- ♥ Lyndon B. Johnson Library and Museum
- ♥ Mary Jo Peckham Park
- ♥ Mayfield Park Cottage and Gardens

- ♥ McNay Art Museum

- ♥ Meadows Museum, Dallas

- ♥ Miller Outdoor Theatre

- ♥ Mount Bonnell

- ♥ Museum of Fine Arts, Houston

- ♥ Mustang Island State Park

- ♥ Mustangs of Las Colinas, Irving

- ♥ Natural Bridge Wildlife Ranch

- ♥ Old Red Courthouse, Dallas

- ♥ Padre Island National Seashore

- ♥ Palace of Wax, Grand Prairie

- ♥ Palo Duro Canyon State Park

- ♥ Rio San Antonio Cruises

- ♥ River Walk, San Antonio

- ♥ Saint Arnold Brewing Company

- ♥ San Antonio Botanical Garden

- ♥ San Antonio Missions National Historical Park

- ♥ San Antonio Zoo

- ♥ Sea Turtle, South Padre Island

- ♥ Sea World San Antonio

- ♥ Shrine of La Virgen De San Juan Del Valle, McAllen

- ♥ Six Flags Fiesta Texas

- ♥ Six Flags Hurricane Harbor, Arlington

- ♥ Snake Farm & Exotic Animal Park, New Braunfels

- ♥ Space Center Houston

- ♥ Stockyards National Historic District

- ♥ Sundance Square, Fort Worth

- ♥ Texas State Aquarium

- ♥ The Bob Bullock Texas State History Museum

- ♥ Times Ten Cellars, Dallas

- ♥ Tower of the Americas

- ♥ Trammell & Margaret Crow Collection of Asian Art

- ♥ Trinity Park, Fort Worth

- ♥ University of Texas Tower

- ♥ Villa De Matel Convent

- ♥ White Rock Lake

- ♥ Zilker Botanical Garden

- ♥ Zilker Park

Things To Do In Utah For Couples

These things to do in Utah offer couples fun inexpensive dates and great date ideas throughout the state.

Utah vacations offer scenic views, skiing, and tours on horseback, ATVs, motorcycles and more.

- ♥ Alpine Slide, Park City

- ♥ Alta Ski Area

- ♥ Antelope Island State Park

- ♥ Artspace Inc., Salt Lake City

- ♥ Beehive House

- ♥ Bingham Canyon Copper Mine

- ♥ Brighton Ski Resort

- ♥ Canyon Trail Rides, Tropic - mule and horseback tour rides

- ♥ Canyons, Park City

- ♥ Castle Country, Price

- ♥ Cathedral of the Madeline

- ♥ Cedar Breaks National Monument

- ♥ Chase Home Museum of Utah Folk Art

- ♥ Church History Museum, Salt Lake City

- ♥ Clark Planetarium

- ♥ Dan Mick's Guided Jeep Tours, Moab

- ♥ Dinosaurland, Vernal

- ♥ Eccles Dinosaur Park

- ♥ Elite Motorcycle Tours, Moab

- ♥ Fort Douglas Military Museum

- ♥ Gardner Village, West Jordan

- ♥ Gilgal Gardens

- ♥ Heber Valley Railroad - scenic rides

- ♥ High Point Hummer & ATV Tours, Moab

- ♥ Hogle Zoo

- ♥ International Peace Gardens

- ♥ Joseph Smith Memorial Building

- ♥ Kingsbury Hall

- ♥ Lagoon, Farmington

- ♥ Liberty Park, Salt Lake City

♥ Monument Valley Navajo Tribal Park

♥ Park City Historic Main Street

♥ Park City Mountain Resort

♥ Park City Museum and Tourist Information Center

♥ Parowan Historical Tour, Cedar City

♥ Pioneer Memorial Museum

♥ Red Butte Gardens

♥ Rockport State Park

♥ Salt Island Adventures - sunset dinner cruise

♥ Sauropod Dinosaur Tracksite, Moab

♥ Seven Peaks Water Park

♥ Snowbird Ski & Summer Resort

♥ Southern Utah Scenic Tours, Cedar City - hike Zion or northern Grand Canyon

♥ Temple Square, Salt Lake City

♥ Thanksgiving Point Gardens

♥ This Is The Place Heritage Park

♥ Timpanogos Cave National Monument, American Fork

♥ Tracy Aviary, Salt Lake

♥ Utah Field House of Natural History State Park

♥ Utah Museum of Fine Arts

♥ Wheeler Historic Farm

Things To Do In Vermont For Couples

Things to do in Vermont for couples. Speak love words, turn up the marriage romance and visit attractions together in the state.

- ♥ Adams Family Farm, Wilmington - teas, sleigh rides, cave exploration
- ♥ Athenaeum Library & Art Gallery, St Johnsbury
- ♥ Ballet Manchester
- ♥ Ben & Jerry's Ice Cream Factory
- ♥ Bike Vermont, Woodstock - tours
- ♥ Bragg Farm Sugarhouse, Montpelier
- ♥ Danforth's Sugarhouse
- ♥ ECHO Lake Aquarium and Science Center
- ♥ Emerald Lake State Park
- ♥ Evergreen Gardens of Vermont
- ♥ Extreme Adventures of Vermont, Ludlow - summer and winter activities
- ♥ Farm at Morrison Corner, Stowe
- ♥ Gallery Walk, Brattleboro
- ♥ Gardens of Seven Gables, Barre
- ♥ Grafton Village Cheese
- ♥ Grand View Winery, Waterbury Center
- ♥ Green Mountain Dog Sled Adventures, Stowe
- ♥ Heritage Winooski Mill Museum
- ♥ Hildene, Manchester
- ♥ Hubbard Park & Tower
- ♥ Lake Champlain Navy Memorial Lone Sailor Statue
- ♥ Lang Farm Nursery, Burlington
- ♥ Little River State Park
- ♥ Lyndon Corn Maze

♥ Mad Tom Orchard, Dorset - have a picnic then pick apples and raspberries

♥ Magic Hat Brewing Company

♥ Martin's Maple Farm, Chester

♥ Morse Farm Maple Sugarworks, Montpelier

♥ Mount Philo State Park

♥ Mountain Meadows Cross Country Skiing

♥ Mountain Valley Farm, Waitsfield - sleigh, wagon and hay rides

♥ Ottauquechee Valley Winery, Woodstock

♥ Paramount Theatre, Rutland

♥ Robb Family Farm & Country Store, Brattleboro

♥ Sand Bar State Park

♥ Shelburne Farms

♥ True North Kayak Tours, Burlington

♥ Vermont State House

♥ Vermont Teddy Bear Company

♥ Winds of Ireland, Burlington - sails on Lake Champlain

Things To Do In Virginia For Couples

Things to do in Virginia for couples. If you're looking at proposing marriage or to rekindle romance, check out these romance ideas and places to see.

♥ Abingdon Historic District

♥ Adam Thoroughgood House, Virginia Beach

♥ Air America, VA Beach - parasail

♥ Algonkian Regional Park

♥ Arcady Vineyard Wine Tours

- ♥ Arlington National Cemetery
- ♥ Bateau River Explorations, Charlottesville
- ♥ Battleship Wisconsin
- ♥ Belvedere Plantation, Fredericksburg
- ♥ Bisset Park, Radford
- ♥ Blackwater Creek Bikeway & Riverwalk
- ♥ Bluebird Gap Farm, Hampton
- ♥ Byrd Theater, Richmond
- ♥ Carrie B. Harbor Tours, Norfolk
- ♥ Chesapeake Arboretum
- ♥ Chrysler Museum of Art
- ♥ Dixie Caverns & Pottery, Salem
- ♥ Falling Spring, Covington
- ♥ Fan District, Richmond
- ♥ Ferry Plantation House, VA Beach
- ♥ Francis Land House, VA Beach
- ♥ George Washington Masonic Memorial
- ♥ Hampton Carousel
- ♥ Haunting Tales, Lexington's Ghost Tour
- ♥ Holy Cross Abbey, Berryville
- ♥ James Madison's Montpelier
- ♥ James River Bridge Fishing Pier, Newport News
- ♥ Kluge Estate Winery & Vineyard
- ♥ Lake Accotink Park, Fairfax

- ♥ Lake Anna State Park

- ♥ Lewis Ginter Botanical Garden

- ♥ Luray Caverns

- ♥ Luray Zoo

- ♥ Manassas National Battlefield Park

- ♥ Meadow Farm Museum, Glen Allen

- ♥ Monticello and the University of Virginia in Charlottesville

- ♥ Monument Avenue, Richmond

- ♥ Mount Vernon

- ♥ Museum of the Confederacy, Richmond

- ♥ Natural Bridge, Roanoke

- ♥ Newport News Park

- ♥ Norfolk Botanical Garden

- ♥ Old Coast Guard Station, Virginia Beach

- ♥ Old Town Alexandria

- ♥ Paramount's Kings Dominion

- ♥ Poe Museum

- ♥ Potomac Overlook Regional Park

- ♥ Richmond Canal Walk

- ♥ Richmond National Battlefield Park

- ♥ Riverside Dinner Theater, Fredericksburg

- ♥ Sandy Bottom Nature Park

- ♥ Shenandoah National Park

- ♥ Shenandoah River Outfitters, Luray - canoe, kayak, tube, fish

- ♥ Shenandoah Valley Discovery Museum

- ♥ Stonewall Jackson House, Lexington

- ♥ The Mariners' Museum, Newport News

- ♥ Theodore Roosevelt Island and Memorial

- ♥ U.S. Marine Corps War Memorial

- ♥ Victory Rover Naval Base Cruises, Norfolk

- ♥ Virginia Air & Space Center

- ♥ Virginia Ballet Theatre

- ♥ Virginia City Gem Mine on Big Walker Mountain

- ♥ Virginia Chorale

- ♥ Virginia Living Museum, Newport News

- ♥ Virginia Safari Park, Lexington

- ♥ Virginia State Capitol

- ♥ Williamsburg Winery

- ♥ Yorktown Victory Center

Washington Attractions For Couples

- ♥ Alki Beach Park

- ♥ Argosy Cruises - dinner cruise

- ♥ Bainbridge Island

- ♥ Bellevue Botanical Garden

- ♥ Cascadian Chorale

- ♥ Center for Wooden Boats, Seattle

- ♥ Chetzemoka Park

- ♥ Chism Beach Park

- ♥ Classic Helicopter Corp - air tour of Seattle

- ♥ Columbia Center

- ♥ Discovery Park

- ♥ Experience Music Project/Science Fiction Museum & Hall of Fame

- ♥ Five Mile Lake

- ♥ Fort Casey State Park

- ♥ Fort Worden State Park

- ♥ Future of Flight Aviation Center & Boeing Tour, Mukilteo

- ♥ Gas Works Park

- ♥ Gene Coulon Memorial Beach Park

- ♥ Hiram M. Chittenden Locks, Seattle

- ♥ Hoh Rain Forest

- ♥ Karpeles Manuscript Library Museum

- ♥ Kelsey Creek Park and Farm

- ♥ Kubota Gardens

- ♥ Marina Park

- ♥ Maritime Pacific Brewing Company and the Jolly Roger Taproom

- ♥ Mount Rainier National Park

- ♥ Mount St. Helens National Volcanic Monument

- ♥ Mt. Baker Ski Area, Bellingham

- ♥ Museum of Flight

- ♥ Museum of Glass, Tacoma

- ♥ Northwest Sinfonietta, Tacoma

- ♥ Odyssey: The Maritime Discovery Center

- ♥ Olympic National Park

- ♥ Pacific Science Center

- ♥ Point Defiance Park, Tacoma

- ♥ Port Townsend

- ♥ Redhook Ale Brewery

- ♥ Ride the Ducks of Seattle

- ♥ Seattle Aquarium

- ♥ Seattle Art Museum

- ♥ Seattle Chinese Garden

- ♥ Seattle Waterfront

- ♥ Seattle's Museum of History & Industry

- ♥ Show Me Seattle

- ♥ Silver Lake Winery

- ♥ Snoqualmie Falls

- ♥ Soos Creek Trail

- ♥ Space Needle

- ♥ Underground Tour, Seattle

- ♥ Washington Park Arboretum

- ♥ Washington Serpentarium

- ♥ Washington State Ferry - see Puget Sound

- ♥ Washington State History Museum

- ♥ Waterfall Gardens, Seattle

- ♥ Western Prince Cruises/Orca Whalewatching, San Juan Island

- ♥ Whale Museum

♥ Whidbey Island

♥ Woodland Park Rose Garden

♥ Woodland Park Zoo

Attractions In Washington DC

These attractions in Washington DC offer couples romantic things to do in DC, romantic ideas for men and women, romantic night ideas and romantic proposals.

♥ Adams-Morgan

♥ Albert Einstein Memorial

♥ Anderson House

♥ Banneker Park

♥ Basilica of the National Shrine of the Immaculate Conception

♥ Bike the Sites - guided bicycle tours

♥ Bureau of Engraving and Printing

♥ Chinatown

♥ Constitution Gardens

♥ Department of State

♥ District of Columbia Arts Center

♥ Dupont Circle

♥ Enid A. Haupt Garden

♥ Farragut Square

♥ Ford's Theatre

♥ Franciscan Monastery

♥ Franklin Delano Roosevelt Memorial

♥ Frederick Douglass National Historic Site

- ♥ Friendship Archway
- ♥ Georgetown
- ♥ Govinda Gallery
- ♥ Hains Point
- ♥ Hillwood House Museum
- ♥ Hirshhorn Museum and Sculpture Garden
- ♥ International Spy Museum
- ♥ John F. Kennedy Center for the Performing Arts
- ♥ Kalorama House and Embassy Tour
- ♥ Keith Lipert Gallery
- ♥ Kenilworth Aquatic Gardens
- ♥ Korean War Veterans Memorial
- ♥ Kreeger Museum
- ♥ Library of Congress
- ♥ Lincoln Memorial
- ♥ Meridian Hill Park
- ♥ Montrose Park
- ♥ National Air and Space Museum
- ♥ National Archives
- ♥ National Building Museum
- ♥ National Gallery of Art
- ♥ National Geographic Museum at Explorers Hall
- ♥ National Law Enforcement Officers Memorial
- ♥ National Mall

- ♥ National Museum of the American Indian
- ♥ National Museum Of The Marine Corps
- ♥ National Museum of Women in the Arts
- ♥ National Portrait Gallery
- ♥ National Postal Museum
- ♥ National World War II Memorial
- ♥ Naval Observatory
- ♥ Octagon Museum
- ♥ Pavilion at the Old Post Office
- ♥ Petersen House
- ♥ Pope John Paul II Cultural Center
- ♥ Reflecting Pool
- ♥ Smithsonian Institution Building
- ♥ Smithsonian National Museum of Natural History
- ♥ Smithsonian National Zoological Park
- ♥ Spirit Cruises - dinner cruise on the Potomac River
- ♥ Textile Museum
- ♥ Thomas Jefferson Memorial
- ♥ Tudor Place
- ♥ Union Station
- ♥ United States Holocaust Memorial Museum
- ♥ United States National Arboretum
- ♥ U.S. Botanic Garden
- ♥ U.S. Capitol Building

- ♥ U.S. Navy Memorial

- ♥ Vietnam Veterans Memorial

- ♥ Washington Harbour

- ♥ Washington Monument

- ♥ Washington National Cathedral

- ♥ White House

- ♥ Woodrow Wilson House

West Virginia Attractions

These West Virginia attractions offer couples romantic date ideas.

Enjoy the beauty of the state with your sweetie on fun and romantic West Virginia vacations.

- ♥ Appalachian Wildwaters, Charleston - white water rafting

- ♥ Augusta Heritage Center, Elkins

- ♥ Beckley Mainstreet

- ♥ Berkeley Springs State Park

- ♥ Blennerhassett Island Historical State Park

- ♥ Capitol Music Hall, Wheeling

- ♥ Comcast Mountain Festival, Bluefield

- ♥ Cranberry Glades Botanical Area, Elkins

- ♥ Hard Rock Climbing Services, Fayetteville

- ♥ Historic Lewisburg - see Carnegie Hall while there

- ♥ Kirkwood Winery

- ♥ Lost World Caverns, Lewisburg

- ♥ Midland Trail National Scenic Byway, Lewisburg

- ♥ Mountain State Mystery Train, Huntington - scenic tours

- ♥ New & Gauley River Adventures

- ♥ New River Gorge Bridge

- ♥ New River Jetboats

- ♥ Oglebay Institute's Towngate Theatre & Cinema

- ♥ Old Brick Playhouse Company, Elkins

- ♥ Old Opera House, Charles Town

- ♥ Prickett's Fort State Park

- ♥ R.C. Marshall Hardware Company, Parkersburg

- ♥ Ridgefield Farm & Orchard, Harpers Ferry - pick apples and pumpkins

- ♥ River Riders, Harpers Ferry - raft, canoe, tube, kayak

- ♥ Smoot Theatre, Parkersburg

- ♥ Valley Falls State Park, Fairmont

- ♥ Victoria Vaudeville Theater, Wheeling

- ♥ West Virginia Independence Hall

- ♥ West Virginia State Capitol Building

Wisconsin Things To Do For Couples

These Wisconsin attractions offer couples romantic evening ideas.

Send your sweetie a few romantic e-cards hinting at a special romance date, then head off and visit a place you both find romantic.

- ♥ Afton Cruise Lines, Hudson

- ♥ Amnicon Falls, Superior

- ♥ Barkhausen Waterfowl Preserve

- ♥ Bay Beach Amusement Park

- ♥ Bay Beach Wildlife Sanctuary
- ♥ Bear Den Petting Zoo & Farm, Racine
- ♥ Brandt's Horse Drawn Wagon & Sleigh Rides, Antigo
- ♥ Bristol Renaissance Faire, Kenosha
- ♥ Cady Cheese Factory
- ♥ Cana Island Lighthouse, Sturgeon Bay
- ♥ Captain Frederick Pabst Mansion
- ♥ Cedar Creek Settlement, Cedarburg
- ♥ Door Peninsula Winery
- ♥ Eagle Cave Natural Park, Spring Green
- ♥ Edelweiss Cruise Dining, Milwaukee
- ♥ Foxfire Gardens, Marshfield
- ♥ Geneva Lake Cruise Line
- ♥ Gibbs Lake, Janesville
- ♥ Gordon Bubolz Nature Preserve
- ♥ Gray's Brewing Company
- ♥ Havenwoods State Forest
- ♥ Hearthstone Historic House Museum, Appleton
- ♥ Henry Vilas Zoo
- ♥ Hidden Trails Corn Maze, Onalaska
- ♥ Hillview Farm Orchard, Eau Claire - pick apples, walk a scenic trail
- ♥ Historic Galloway House and Village, Fond du Lac
- ♥ Historic Octagon House & Costume Closet, Fond du Lac
- ♥ House on the Rock, Dodgeville

- ♥ Iverson Park, Stevens Point
- ♥ La Crosse Queen Cruises - dinner cruise
- ♥ Lac Lawrann Conservancy
- ♥ Lake Wissota State Park
- ♥ M&M Ranch, Sparta
- ♥ Marinette County Waterfall Tour
- ♥ Miller Brewing Company
- ♥ Milwaukee County Zoo
- ♥ New Glarus Brewing
- ♥ Noah's Ark Water Park
- ♥ Northern Lights Playhouse, Woodruff
- ♥ Original Wisconsin Ducks
- ♥ Peck's Wildwood Wildlife Park
- ♥ Peninsula State Park
- ♥ Pleasure Valley Llamas, Sheboygan
- ♥ Racine Zoological Gardens
- ♥ Redrock Trail Rides, Sparta
- ♥ River Bend Nature Center, Racine
- ♥ Riverside & Great Northern Preservation Society
- ♥ Roehrborn's Berry Patch, Marshfield - pick strawberries
- ♥ Rudolph Grotto Gardens & Wonder Cave
- ♥ Saint Rose Convent, La Crosse
- ♥ Sea Dog Sailing, Milwaukee - on Lake Michigan
- ♥ Shalom Wildlife Sanctuary

♥ Sugar River State Trail, New Glarus

♥ The Farm, Sturgeon Bay

♥ Triangle Sports Area, Green Bay

♥ Watson's Wild West Museum

♥ Whitnall Park

♥ Wilderness Walk Zoo and Recreation

♥ Wildwood Park & Zoo, Marshfield

♥ Wind Point Lighthouse, Racine

♥ Wisconsin State Capital Building

Things To Do In Wyoming For Couples

Things to do in Wyoming for couples offer romantic ideas for dates, romantic picnic ideas, winter date ideas and a few unusual dates!

Romantic gestures and words are key to healthy relationships, so head off and enjoy fun Wyoming vacations.

♥ A&W Bowling Center, Thermopolis

♥ Audubon Center at Garden Creek, Casper

♥ Ayers Natural Bridge, Douglas

♥ Bar T-5 Covered Wagon Cookout and Show, Jackson

♥ Bear River State Park

♥ Botanic Gardens, Cheyenne

♥ Casper Ghosts Professional Baseball Club

♥ Casper Ice Arena

♥ Central Wyoming Fair & Rodeo - each July

♥ Cheyenne Symphony Orchestra

♥ Cloud Peak Ferris Wheel, Buffalo

- ♥ Cowboy Carousel, Buffalo
- ♥ Douglas Motorsports Park - drag racing
- ♥ Douglas Railroad Interpretive Center
- ♥ Eagle Butte, Gillette
- ♥ Evanston Cowboy Days - Labor Day weekend
- ♥ Evanston Rodeo Series - every June
- ♥ Fort Caspar Museum & Historic Site
- ♥ Historic Governors' Mansion
- ♥ IKON Center, Cheyenne
- ♥ Jackson Hole Mountain Guides - hike, backpack, rock climb
- ♥ Jackson Hole Wine Auction
- ♥ Jubilee Days, Laramie - every July
- ♥ Lewis & Clark River Expeditions, Jackson
- ♥ Memory Lanes, Rawlins
- ♥ Miniature Golf, Buffalo
- ♥ National Bighorn Sheep Interpretive Center, Dubois
- ♥ Prairie Rides, Laramie - fish, sight see, tours
- ♥ Putt Putt Golf, Casper
- ♥ Red Canyon River Trips
- ♥ River Runners, Cody - rafting
- ♥ Spirit Mountain Aviation, Inc., Cody - scenic flights
- ♥ Three Quarter Circle Ranch, Lander
- ♥ Trail End State Historic Site, Sheridan
- ♥ Uinta County Fair, Evanston

- ♥ Western Encounters, Lander - horse trips

- ♥ Wyoming Cavalry

- ♥ Wyoming Symphony Orchestra

ABOUT THE AUTHOR

K. M. Ryan is the writer and publisher of eight websites including Lots of Romantic Ideas.com, Best US Romantic Getaways.com and Vacation Wedding Ideas.com.

Her other books include "Greetings From Above, Proof of Life After Death" and "Women, Men and Relationships."

She holds a Master's Degree, is active in her church, and on the Alumni Board of Directors at her alma mater.

Made in the USA
Lexington, KY
09 January 2014